THE MERRY WIVES OF WINDSOR

THE MERRY WIVES OF WINDSOR

WILLIAM SHAKESPEARE

ISBN: 978-93-5344-300-9

First Published: -

LECTOR HOUSE LLP
E-MAIL: lectorpublishing@gmail.com

THE MERRY WIVES
OF WINDSOR

BY

WILLIAM SHAKESPEARE

CONTENTS

ACT V

DRAMATIS PERSONAE

SIR JOHN FALSTAFF
FENTON, a young gentleman
SHALLOW, a country justice
SLENDER, cousin to Shallow
FORD, a Gentleman dwelling at Windsor
PAGE, a Gentleman dwelling at Windsor
WILLIAM PAGE, a boy, son to Page
SIR HUGH EVANS, a Welsh parson
DOCTOR CAIUS, a French physician
HOST of the Garter Inn
BARDOLPH, **PISTOL**, **NYM;** Followers of Falstaff
ROBIN, page to Falstaff
SIMPLE, servant to Slender
RUGBY, servant to Doctor Caius

MISTRESS FORD
MISTRESS PAGE
MISTRESS ANNE PAGE, her daughter, in love with Fenton
MISTRESS QUICKLY, servant to Doctor Caius

SERVANTS to Page, Ford, &c

SCENE: Windsor and the neighbourhood

ACT I

SCENE I.

WINDSOR. BEFORE PAGE'S HOUSE

[Enter JUSTICE SHALLOW, SLENDER, and SIR HUGH EVANS.]

SHALLOW
Sir Hugh, persuade me not; I will make a Star Chamber matter of it; if he were twenty Sir John Falstaffs, he shall not abuse Robert Shallow, esquire.

SLENDER
In the county of Gloucester, Justice of Peace, and "coram."

SHALLOW
Ay, cousin Slender, and "cust-alorum."

SLENDER
Ay, and "rato-lorum" too; and a gentleman born, Master Parson, who writes himself "armigero" in any bill, warrant, quittance, or obligation — "armigero."

SHALLOW
Ay, that I do; and have done any time these three hundred years.

SLENDER
All his successors, gone before him, hath done't; and all his ancestors, that come after him, may: they may give the dozen white luces in their coat.

SHALLOW
It is an old coat.

EVANS
The dozen white louses do become an old coat well; it agrees well, passant; it is a familiar beast to man, and signifies love.

SHALLOW
The luce is the fresh fish; the salt fish is an old coat.

SLENDER
I may quarter, coz?

SHALLOW
You may, by marrying.

EVANS
It is marring indeed, if he quarter it.

SHALLOW
Not a whit.

EVANS
Yes, py'r lady! If he has a quarter of your coat, there is but three skirts for yourself, in my simple conjectures; but that is all one. If Sir John Falstaff have committed disparagements unto you, I am of the church, and will be glad to do my benevolence to make atonements and compremises between you.

SHALLOW
The Council shall hear it; it is a riot.

EVANS
It is not meet the Council hear a riot; there is no fear of Got in a riot; the Council, look you, shall desire to hear the fear of Got, and not to hear a riot; take your vizaments in that.

SHALLOW
Ha! o' my life, if I were young again, the sword should end it.

EVANS
It is petter that friends is the sword and end it; and there is also another device in my prain, which peradventure prings goot discretions with it. There is Anne Page, which is daughter to Master George Page, which is pretty virginity.

SLENDER
Mistress Anne Page? She has brown hair, and speaks small like a woman.

EVANS
It is that fery person for all the orld, as just as you will desire; and seven hundred pounds of moneys, and gold, and silver, is her grandsire upon his death's-bed — Got deliver to a joyful resurrections! — give, when she is able to overtake seventeen years old. It were a goot motion if we leave our pribbles and prabbles, and desire a marriage between Master Abra-

ham and Mistress Anne Page.

SHALLOW
Did her grandsire leave her seven hundred pound?

EVANS
Ay, and her father is make her a petter penny.

SHALLOW
I know the young gentlewoman; she has good gifts.

EVANS
Seven hundred pounds, and possibilities, is goot gifts.

SHALLOW
Well, let us see honest Master Page. Is Falstaff there?

EVANS
Shall I tell you a lie? I do despise a liar as I do despise one that is false;
or as I despise one that is not true. The knight Sir John is there; and, I beseech you, be ruled by your well-willers. I will peat the door for Master
Page.

[Knocks.]

What, hoa! Got pless your house here!

PAGE
[Within] Who's there?

EVANS
Here is Got's plessing, and your friend, and Justice Shallow; and here
young Master Slender, that peradventures shall tell you another tale, if
matters grow to your likings.

[Enter PAGE.]

PAGE
I am glad to see your worships well. I thank you for my venison, Master
Shallow.

SHALLOW
Master Page, I am glad to see you; much good do it your good heart! I
wished your venison better; it was ill killed. How doth good Mistress
Page? — and I thank you always with my heart, la! with my heart.

PAGE
Sir, I thank you.

SHALLOW
Sir, I thank you; by yea and no, I do.

PAGE
I am glad to see you, good Master Slender.

SLENDER
How does your fallow greyhound, sir? I heard say he was outrun on Cot-sall.

PAGE
It could not be judged, sir.

SLENDER
You'll not confess, you'll not confess.

SHALLOW
That he will not: 'tis your fault; 'tis your fault. 'Tis a good dog.

PAGE
A cur, sir.

SHALLOW
Sir, he's a good dog, and a fair dog; can there be more said? he is good, and fair. Is Sir John Falstaff here?

PAGE
Sir, he is within; and I would I could do a good office between you.

EVANS
It is spoke as a Christians ought to speak.

SHALLOW
He hath wronged me, Master Page.

PAGE
Sir, he doth in some sort confess it.

SHALLOW
If it be confessed, it is not redressed: is not that so, Master Page? He hath wronged me; indeed he hath; — at a word, he hath, — believe me; Robert Shallow, esquire, saith he is wronged.

PAGE
Here comes Sir John.

[Enter SIR JOHN FALSTAFF, BARDOLPH, NYM, and PISTOL.]

FALSTAFF
Now, Master Shallow, you'll complain of me to the King?

SHALLOW
Knight, you have beaten my men, killed my deer, and broke open my lodge.

FALSTAFF
But not kiss'd your keeper's daughter?

SHALLOW
Tut, a pin! this shall be answered.

FALSTAFF
I will answer it straight: I have done all this. That is now answered.

SHALLOW
The Council shall know this.

FALSTAFF
'Twere better for you if it were known in counsel: you'll be laughed at.

EVANS
Pauca verba, Sir John; goot worts.

FALSTAFF
Good worts! good cabbage! Slender, I broke your head; what matter have you against me?

SLENDER
Marry, sir, I have matter in my head against you; and against your co-ny-catching rascals, Bardolph, Nym, and Pistol. They carried me to the tavern, and made me drunk, and afterwards picked my pocket.

BARDOLPH
You Banbury cheese!

SLENDER
Ay, it is no matter.

PISTOL
How now, Mephostophilus!

SLENDER
Ay, it is no matter.

NYM
Slice, I say! pauca, pauca; slice! That's my humour.

SLENDER
Where's Simple, my man? Can you tell, cousin?

EVANS
Peace, I pray you. Now let us understand. There is three umpires in this matter, as I understand: that is — Master Page, fidelicet Master Page; and there is myself, fidelicet myself; and the three party is, lastly and finally, mine host of the Garter.

PAGE
We three to hear it and end it between them.

EVANS
Fery goot: I will make a prief of it in my note-book; and we will after-wards ork upon the cause with as great discreetly as we can.

FALSTAFF
Pistol!

PISTOL
He hears with ears.

EVANS
The tevil and his tam! what phrase is this, "He hears with ear"? Why, it is affectations.

FALSTAFF
Pistol, did you pick Master Slender's purse?

SLENDER
Ay, by these gloves, did he — or I would I might never come in mine own great chamber again else! — of seven groats in mill-sixpences, and two Edward shovel-boards that cost me two shilling and two pence a-piece of Yead Miller, by these gloves.

FALSTAFF
Is this true, Pistol?

EVANS
No, it is false, if it is a pick-purse.

PISTOL
Ha, thou mountain-foreigner! — Sir John and master mine,

I combat challenge of this latten bilbo.
Word of denial in thy labras here!
Word of denial! Froth and scum, thou liest.

SLENDER
By these gloves, then, 'twas he.

NYM
Be avised, sir, and pass good humours; I will say "marry trap" with you,
if you run the nuthook's humour on me; that is the very note of it.

SLENDER
By this hat, then, he in the red face had it; for though I cannot remember
what I did when you made me drunk, yet I am not altogether an ass.

FALSTAFF
What say you, Scarlet and John?

BARDOLPH
Why, sir, for my part, I say the gentleman had drunk himself out of his
five sentences.

EVANS
It is his "five senses"; fie, what the ignorance is!

BARDOLPH
And being fap, sir, was, as they say, cashier'd; and so conclusions passed
the careires.

SLENDER
Ay, you spake in Latin then too; but 'tis no matter; I'll ne'er be drunk
whilst I live again, but in honest, civil, godly company, for this trick; if I
be drunk, I'll be drunk with those that have the fear of God, and not with
drunken knaves.

EVANS
So Got udge me, that is a virtuous mind.

FALSTAFF
You hear all these matters denied, gentlemen; you hear it.

*[Enter ANNE PAGE with wine; MISTRESS FORD and MISTRESS PAGE,
following.]*

PAGE
Nay, daughter, carry the wine in; we'll drink within.

[Exit ANNE PAGE.]

SLENDER
O heaven! this is Mistress Anne Page.

PAGE
How now, Mistress Ford!

FALSTAFF
Mistress Ford, by my troth, you are very well met; by your leave, good
mistress. [Kissing her]

PAGE
Wife, bid these gentlemen welcome. Come, we have a hot venison pasty
to dinner; come, gentlemen, I hope we shall drink down all unkindness.

[Exeunt all but SHALLOW, SLENDER, and EVANS.]

SLENDER
I had rather than forty shillings I had my Book of Songs and Sonnets
here.

[Enter SIMPLE.]

How, Simple! Where have you been? I must wait on myself, must I? You
have not the Book of Riddles about you, have you?

SIMPLE
Book of Riddles! why, did you not lend it to Alice Shortcake upon Allhal-
lowmas last, a fortnight afore Michaelmas?

SHALLOW
Come, coz; come, coz; we stay for you. A word with you, coz; marry,
this, coz: there is, as 'twere, a tender, a kind of tender, made afar off by
Sir Hugh here: do you understand me?

SLENDER
Ay, sir, you shall find me reasonable; if it be so, I shall do that that is
reason.

SHALLOW
Nay, but understand me.

SLENDER
So I do, sir.

EVANS
Give ear to his motions, Master Slender: I will description the matter to
you, if you pe capacity of it.

SLENDER

Nay, I will do as my cousin Shallow says; I pray you pardon me; he's a justice of peace in his country, simple though I stand here.

EVANS
But that is not the question; the question is concerning your marriage.

SHALLOW
Ay, there's the point, sir.

EVANS
Marry is it; the very point of it; to Mistress Anne Page.

SLENDER
Why, if it be so, I will marry her upon any reasonable demands.

EVANS
But can you affection the 'oman? Let us command to know that of your mouth or of your lips; for divers philosophers hold that the lips is parcel of the mouth: therefore, precisely, can you carry your good will to the maid?

SHALLOW
Cousin Abraham Slender, can you love her?

SLENDER
I hope, sir, I will do as it shall become one that would do reason.

EVANS
Nay, Got's lords and his ladies! you must speak possitable, if you can carry her your desires towards her.

SHALLOW
That you must. Will you, upon good dowry, marry her?

SLENDER
I will do a greater thing than that upon your request, cousin, in any reason.

SHALLOW
Nay, conceive me, conceive me, sweet coz; what I do is to pleasure you, coz. Can you love the maid?

SLENDER
I will marry her, sir, at your request; but if there be no great love in the beginning, yet heaven may decrease it upon better acquaintance, when we are married and have more occasion to know one another; I hope

upon familiarity will grow more contempt. But if you say "Marry her," I will marry her; that I am freely dissolved, and dissolutely.

EVANS
It is a fery discretion answer; save, the fall is in the ort "dissolutely:" the ort is, according to our meaning, "resolutely." His meaning is good.

SHALLOW
Ay, I think my cousin meant well.

SLENDER
Ay, or else I would I might be hanged, la!

SHALLOW
Here comes fair Mistress Anne.

[Re-enter ANNE PAGE.]

Would I were young for your sake, Mistress Anne!

ANNE
The dinner is on the table; my father desires your worships' company.

SHALLOW
I will wait on him, fair Mistress Anne!

EVANS
Od's plessed will! I will not be absence at the grace.

[Exeunt SHALLOW and EVANS.]

ANNE
Will't please your worship to come in, sir?

SLENDER
No, I thank you, forsooth, heartily; I am very well.

ANNE
The dinner attends you, sir.

SLENDER
I am not a-hungry, I thank you, forsooth. Go, sirrah, for all you are my man, go wait upon my cousin Shallow.

[Exit SIMPLE.]

A justice of peace sometime may be beholding to his friend for a man. I keep but three men and a boy yet, till my mother be dead. But what though? Yet I live like a poor gentleman born.

ANNE
I may not go in without your worship: they will not sit till you come.

SLENDER
I' faith, I'll eat nothing; I thank you as much as though I did.

ANNE
I pray you, sir, walk in.

SLENDER
I had rather walk here, I thank you. I bruised my shin th' other day with playing at sword and dagger with a master of fence; three veneys for a dish of stewed prunes — and, by my troth, I cannot abide the smell of hot meat since. Why do your dogs bark so? Be there bears i› the town?

ANNE
I think there are, sir; I heard them talked of.

SLENDER
I love the sport well; but I shall as soon quarrel at it as any man in England. You are afraid, if you see the bear loose, are you not?

ANNE
Ay, indeed, sir.

SLENDER
That's meat and drink to me now. I have seen Sackerson loose twenty times, and have taken him by the chain; but I warrant you, the women have so cried and shrieked at it that it passed; but women, indeed, cannot abide 'em; they are very ill-favoured rough things.

[Re-enter PAGE.]

PAGE
Come, gentle Master Slender, come; we stay for you.

SLENDER
I'll eat nothing, I thank you, sir.

PAGE
By cock and pie, you shall not choose, sir! come, come.

SLENDER
Nay, pray you lead the way.

PAGE
Come on, sir.

SLENDER
Mistress Anne, yourself shall go first.

ANNE
Not I, sir; pray you keep on.

SLENDER
Truly, I will not go first; truly, la! I will not do you that wrong.

ANNE
I pray you, sir.

SLENDER
I'll rather be unmannerly than troublesome. You do yourself wrong indeed, la!

[Exeunt.]

SCENE II.

THE SAME

[Enter SIR HUGH EVANS and SIMPLE.]

EVANS
Go your ways, and ask of Doctor Caius' house which is the way; and
there dwells one Mistress Quickly, which is in the manner of his nurse,
or his dry nurse, or his cook, or his laundry, his washer, and his wringer.

SIMPLE
Well, sir.

EVANS
Nay, it is petter yet. Give her this letter; for it is a 'oman that altogether's
acquaintance with Mistress Anne Page; and the letter is to desire and
require her to solicit your master's desires to Mistress Anne Page. I pray
you be gone: I will make an end of my dinner; there's pippins and cheese
to come.

[Exeunt.]

SCENE III.

A ROOM IN THE GARTER INN

[Enter FALSTAFF, HOST, BARDOLPH, NYM, PISTOL, and ROBIN.]

FALSTAFF
Mine host of the Garter!

HOST
What says my bully rook? Speak scholarly and wisely.

FALSTAFF
Truly, mine host, I must turn away some of my followers.

HOST
Discard, bully Hercules; cashier; let them wag; trot, trot.

FALSTAFF
I sit at ten pounds a week.

HOST
Thou'rt an emperor, Caesar, Keiser, and Pheazar. I will entertain Bardolph; he shall draw, he shall tap; said I well, bully Hector?

FALSTAFF
Do so, good mine host.

HOST
I have spoke; let him follow. *[To BARDOLPH]* Let me see thee froth and
lime. I am at a word; follow.

[Exit HOST.]

FALSTAFF
Bardolph, follow him. A tapster is a good trade; an old cloak makes a
new jerkin; a withered serving-man a fresh tapster. Go; adieu.

BARDOLPH
It is a life that I have desired; I will thrive.

PISTOL
O base Hungarian wight! Wilt thou the spigot wield?

[Exit BARDOLPH.]

NYM
He was gotten in drink. Is not the humour conceited?

FALSTAFF
I am glad I am so acquit of this tinder-box: his thefts were too open; his filching was like an unskilful singer — he kept not time.

NYM
The good humour is to steal at a minim's rest.

PISTOL
"Convey" the wise it call. "Steal!" foh! A fico for the phrase!

FALSTAFF
Well, sirs, I am almost out at heels.

PISTOL
Why, then, let kibes ensue.

FALSTAFF
There is no remedy; I must cony-catch; I must shift.

PISTOL
Young ravens must have food.

FALSTAFF
Which of you know Ford of this town?

PISTOL
I ken the wight; he is of substance good.

FALSTAFF
My honest lads, I will tell you what I am about.

PISTOL
Two yards, and more.

FALSTAFF
No quips now, Pistol. Indeed, I am in the waist two yards about; but I am now about no waste; I am about thrift. Briefly, I do mean to make love to Ford's wife; I spy entertainment in her; she discourses, she carves, she gives the leer of invitation; I can construe the action of her familiar style;

and the hardest voice of her behaviour, to be Englished rightly, is "I am Sir John Falstaff's."

PISTOL
He hath studied her will, and translated her will out of honesty into English.

NYM
The anchor is deep; will that humour pass?

FALSTAFF
Now, the report goes she has all the rule of her husband's purse; he hath a legion of angels.

PISTOL
As many devils entertain; and "To her, boy," say I.

NYM
The humour rises; it is good; humour me the angels.

FALSTAFF
I have writ me here a letter to her; and here another to Page's wife, who even now gave me good eyes too, examined my parts with most judicious oeillades; sometimes the beam of her view gilded my foot, sometimes my portly belly.

PISTOL
Then did the sun on dunghill shine.

NYM
I thank thee for that humour.

FALSTAFF
O! she did so course o'er my exteriors with such a greedy intention that the appetite of her eye did seem to scorch me up like a burning-glass. Here's another letter to her: she bears the purse too; she is a region in Guiana, all gold and bounty. I will be cheator to them both, and they shall be exchequers to me; they shall be my East and West Indies, and I will trade to them both. Go, bear thou this letter to Mistress Page; and thou this to Mistress Ford. We will thrive, lads, we will thrive.

PISTOL
Shall I Sir Pandarus of Troy become,
And by my side wear steel? then Lucifer take all!

NYM

I will run no base humour. Here, take the humour-letter; I will keep the
haviour of reputation.

FALSTAFF
[To ROBIN] Hold, sirrah; bear you these letters tightly;
Sail like my pinnace to these golden shores.
Rogues, hence, avaunt! vanish like hailstones, go;
Trudge, plod away o' hoof; seek shelter, pack!
Falstaff will learn the humour of this age;
French thrift, you rogues; myself, and skirted page.

[Exeunt FALSTAFF and ROBIN.]

PISTOL
Let vultures gripe thy guts! for gourd and fullam holds,
And high and low beguile the rich and poor;
Tester I'll have in pouch when thou shalt lack,
Base Phrygian Turk!

NYM
I have operations in my head which be humours of revenge.

PISTOL
Wilt thou revenge?

NYM
By welkin and her star!

PISTOL
With wit or steel?

NYM
With both the humours, I:
I will discuss the humour of this love to Page.

PISTOL
And I to Ford shall eke unfold
How Falstaff, varlet vile,
His dove will prove, his gold will hold,
And his soft couch defile.

NYM
My humour shall not cool: I will incense Page to deal with poison; I will
possess him with yellowness, for the revolt of mine is dangerous: that is
my true humour.

PISTOL

Thou art the Mars of malcontents; I second thee; troop on.

[Exeunt.]

SCENE IV.

A ROOM IN DOCTOR CAIUS'S HOUSE

[Enter MISTRESS QUICKLY, and SIMPLE.]

QUICKLY
What, John Rugby!

[Enter RUGBY.]

I pray thee go to the casement, and see if you can see my master, Master Doctor Caius, coming: if he do, i' faith, and find anybody in the house, here will be an old abusing of God's patience and the King's English.

RUGBY
I'll go watch.

QUICKLY
Go; and we'll have a posset for't soon at night, in faith, at the latter end of a sea-coal fire.

[Exit RUGBY.]

An honest, willing, kind fellow, as ever servant shall come in house withal; and, I warrant you, no tell-tale nor no breed-bate; his worst fault is that he is given to prayer; he is something peevish that way; but nobody but has his fault; but let that pass. Peter Simple you say your name is?

SIMPLE
Ay, for fault of a better.

QUICKLY
And Master Slender's your master?

SIMPLE
Ay, forsooth.

QUICKLY
Does he not wear a great round beard, like a glover's paring-knife?

SIMPLE
No, forsooth; he hath but a little whey face, with a little yellow beard — a

cane-coloured beard.

QUICKLY
A softly-sprighted man, is he not?

SIMPLE
Ay, forsooth; but he is as tall a man of his hands as any is between this
and his head; he hath fought with a warrener.

QUICKLY
How say you? — O! I should remember him. Does he not hold up his
head, as it were, and strut in his gait?

SIMPLE
Yes, indeed, does he.

QUICKLY
Well, heaven send Anne Page no worse fortune! Tell Master Parson
Evans I will do what I can for your master: Anne is a good girl, and I
wish —

[Re-enter RUGBY.]

RUGBY
Out, alas! here comes my master.

QUICKLY
We shall all be shent. Run in here, good young man; go into this closet.

[Shuts SIMPLE in the closet.]

He will not stay long. What, John Rugby! John! what, John, I say! Go,
John, go inquire for my master; I doubt he be not well that he comes not
home.

[Exit Rugby.]

[Sings.] And down, down, adown-a, &c.

[Enter DOCTOR CAIUS.]

CAIUS
Vat is you sing? I do not like des toys. Pray you, go and vetch me in my
closet une boitine verde — a box, a green-a box: do intend vat I speak? a
green-a box.

QUICKLY
Ay, forsooth, I'll fetch it you.
[Aside] I am glad he went not in himself: if he had found the young man,
he would have been horn-mad.

CAIUS
Fe, fe, fe fe! ma foi, il fait fort chaud. Je m'en vais a la cour — la grande affaire.

QUICKLY
Is it this, sir?

CAIUS
Oui; mettez le au mon pocket: depechez, quickly — Vere is dat knave, Rugby?

QUICKLY
What, John Rugby? John!

[Re-enter Rugby.]

RUGBY
Here, sir.

CAIUS
You are John Rugby, and you are Jack Rugby: come, take-a your rapier, and come after my heel to de court.

RUGBY
'Tis ready, sir, here in the porch.

CAIUS
By my trot, I tarry too long — Od's me! Qu'ay j'oublie? Dere is some simples in my closet dat I vill not for the varld I shall leave behind.

QUICKLY
[Aside] Ay me, he'll find the young man there, and be mad!

CAIUS
O diable, diable! vat is in my closet? — Villainy! larron!

[Pulling SIMPLE out]

Rugby, my rapier!

QUICKLY
Good master, be content.

CAIUS
Verefore shall I be content-a?

QUICKLY
The young man is an honest man.

CAIUS
What shall de honest man do in my closet? dere is no honest man dat shall come in my closet.

QUICKLY
I beseech you, be not so phlegmatic. Hear the truth of it: he came of an errand to me from Parson Hugh.

CAIUS
Vell.

SIMPLE
Ay, forsooth, to desire her to —

QUICKLY
Peace, I pray you.

CAIUS
Peace-a your tongue! — Speak-a your tale.

SIMPLE
To desire this honest gentlewoman, your maid, to speak a good word to Mistress Anne Page for my master, in the way of marriage.

QUICKLY
This is all, indeed, la! but I'll ne'er put my finger in the fire, and need not.

CAIUS
Sir Hugh send-a you? — Rugby, baillez me some paper: tarry you a little-a while. [Writes.]

QUICKLY
I am glad he is so quiet: if he had been throughly moved, you should have heard him so loud and so melancholy. But notwithstanding, man, I'll do you your master what good I can; and the very yea and the no is, the French doctor, my master — I may call him my master, look you, for I keep his house; and I wash, wring, brew, bake, scour, dress meat and drink, make the beds, and do all myself —

SIMPLE
'Tis a great charge to come under one body's hand.

QUICKLY
Are you avis'd o' that? You shall find it a great charge; and to be up early and down late; but notwithstanding, — to tell you in your ear, — I would have no words of it — my master himself is in love with Mistress

Anne Page; but notwithstanding that, I know Anne's mind, that's neither here nor there.

CAIUS
You jack'nape; give-a dis letter to Sir Hugh; by gar, it is a shallenge: I will cut his troat in de Park; and I will teach a scurvy jack-a-nape priest to meddle or make. You may be gone; it is not good you tarry here: by gar, I will cut all his two stones; by gar, he shall not have a stone to throw at his dog.

[Exit SIMPLE.]

QUICKLY
Alas, he speaks but for his friend.

CAIUS
It is no matter-a ver dat: — do not you tell-a me dat I shall have Anne Page for myself? By gar, I vill kill de Jack priest; and I have appointed mine host of de Jartiere to measure our weapon. By gar, I vill myself have Anne Page.

QUICKLY
Sir, the maid loves you, and all shall be well. We must give folks leave to prate: what, the good-jer!

CAIUS
Rugby, come to the court vit me. By gar, if I have not Anne Page, I shall turn your head out of my door. Follow my heels, Rugby.

[Exeunt CAIUS and RUGBY.]

QUICKLY
You shall have An fool's-head of your own. No, I know Anne's mind for that: never a woman in Windsor knows more of Anne's mind than I do; nor can do more than I do with her, I thank heaven.

FENTON
[Within]
Who's within there? ho!

QUICKLY
Who's there, I trow? Come near the house, I pray you.

[Enter FENTON.]

FENTON
How now, good woman! how dost thou?

QUICKLY

The better, that it pleases your good worship to ask.

FENTON
What news? how does pretty Mistress Anne?

QUICKLY
In truth, sir, and she is pretty, and honest, and gentle; and one that is your friend, I can tell you that by the way; I praise heaven for it.

FENTON
Shall I do any good, thinkest thou? Shall I not lose my suit?

QUICKLY
Troth, sir, all is in His hands above; but notwithstanding, Master Fenton, I'll be sworn on a book she loves you. Have not your worship a wart above your eye?

FENTON
Yes, marry, have I; what of that?

QUICKLY
Well, thereby hangs a tale; good faith, it is such another Nan; but, I detest, an honest maid as ever broke bread. We had an hour's talk of that wart; I shall never laugh but in that maid's company; — but, indeed, she is given too much to allicholy and musing. But for you — well, go to.

FENTON
Well, I shall see her to-day. Hold, there's money for thee; let me have thy voice in my behalf: if thou seest her before me, commend me.

QUICKLY
Will I? i' faith, that we will; and I will tell your worship more of the wart the next time we have confidence; and of other wooers.

FENTON
Well, farewell; I am in great haste now.

QUICKLY
Farewell to your worship. —
[Exit FENTON.]

Truly, an honest gentleman; but Anne loves him not; for I know Anne's mind as well as another does. Out upon 't, what have I forgot?
[Exit.]

ACT II.

SCENE I.

BEFORE PAGE'S HOUSE

[Enter MISTRESS PAGE, with a letter.]

MRS. PAGE
What! have I scaped love-letters in the holiday-time of my beauty, and am I now a subject for them? Let me see.

"Ask me no reason why I love you; for though Love use Reason for his precisian, he admits him not for his counsellor. You are not young, no more am I; go to, then, there's sympathy: you are merry, so am I; ha! ha! then there's more sympathy; you love sack, and so do I; would you desire better sympathy? Let it suffice thee, Mistress Page, at the least, if the love of soldier can suffice, that I love thee. I will not say, pity me: 'tis not a soldier-like phrase; but I say, Love me. By me,
Thine own true knight,
By day or night,
Or any kind of light,
With all his might,
For thee to fight,
JOHN FALSTAFF."

What a Herod of Jewry is this! O wicked, wicked world! One that is well-nigh worn to pieces with age to show himself a young gallant. What an unweighed behaviour hath this Flemish drunkard picked, with the devil's name! out of my conversation, that he dares in this manner assay me? Why, he hath not been thrice in my company! What should I say to him? I was then frugal of my mirth: — Heaven forgive me! Why, I'll exhibit a bill in the parliament for the putting down of men. How shall I be revenged on him? for revenged I will be, as sure as his guts are made of puddings.

[Enter MISTRESS FORD.]

MRS. FORD
Mistress Page! trust me, I was going to your house.

MRS. PAGE
And, trust me, I was coming to you. You look very ill.

MRS. FORD
Nay, I'll ne'er believe that; I have to show to the contrary.

MRS. PAGE
Faith, but you do, in my mind.

MRS. FORD
Well, I do, then; yet, I say, I could show you to the contrary. O, Mistress Page! give me some counsel.

MRS. PAGE
What's the matter, woman?

MRS. FORD
O woman, if it were not for one trifling respect, I could come to such honour!

MRS. PAGE
Hang the trifle, woman; take the honour. What is it? — Dispense with trifles; — what is it?

MRS. FORD
If I would but go to hell for an eternal moment or so, I could be knighted.

MRS. PAGE
What? thou liest. Sir Alice Ford! These knights will hack; and so thou shouldst not alter the article of thy gentry.

MRS. FORD
We burn daylight: here, read, read; perceive how I might be knighted. I shall think the worse of fat men as long as I have an eye to make difference of men's liking: and yet he would not swear; praised women's modesty; and gave such orderly and well-behaved reproof to all uncomeliness that I would have sworn his disposition would have gone to the truth of his words; but they do no more adhere and keep place together than the Hundredth Psalm to the tune of "Greensleeves." What tempest, I trow, threw this whale, with so many tuns of oil in his belly, ashore at Windsor? How shall I be revenged on him? I think the best way were to entertain him with hope, till the wicked fire of lust have melted him in his own grease. Did you ever hear the like?

MRS. PAGE
Letter for letter, but that the name of Page and Ford differs. To thy great comfort in this mystery of ill opinions, here's the twin-brother of thy letter; but let thine inherit first, for, I protest, mine never shall. I warrant he hath a thousand of these letters, writ with blank space for different

names, sure, more, and these are of the second edition. He will print
them, out of doubt; for he cares not what he puts into the press, when he
would put us two: I had rather be a giantess and lie under Mount Pelion.
Well, I will find you twenty lascivious turtles ere one chaste man.

MRS. FORD
Why, this is the very same; the very hand, the very words. What doth he
think of us?

MRS. PAGE
Nay, I know not; it makes me almost ready to wrangle with mine own
honesty. I'll entertain myself like one that I am not acquainted withal; for,
sure, unless he know some strain in me that I know not myself, he would
never have boarded me in this fury.

MRS. FORD
"Boarding" call you it? I'll be sure to keep him above deck.

MRS. PAGE
So will I; if he come under my hatches, I'll never to sea again. Let's be revenged on him; let's appoint him a meeting, give him a show of comfort
in his suit, and lead him on with a fine-baited delay, till he hath pawned
his horses to mine host of the Garter.

MRS. FORD
Nay, I will consent to act any villainy against him that may not sully the
chariness of our honesty. O, that my husband saw this letter! It would
give eternal food to his jealousy.

MRS. PAGE
Why, look where he comes; and my good man too: he's as far from jealousy as I am from giving him cause; and that, I hope, is an unmeasurable
distance.

MRS. FORD
You are the happier woman.

MRS. PAGE
Let's consult together against this greasy knight. Come hither.

[They retire.]

[Enter FORD, PISTOL, and PAGE and NYM.]

FORD
Well, I hope it be not so.

PISTOL

Hope is a curtal dog in some affairs:
Sir John affects thy wife.

FORD
Why, sir, my wife is not young.

PISTOL
He woos both high and low, both rich and poor,
Both young and old, one with another, Ford;
He loves the gallimaufry. Ford, perpend.

FORD
Love my wife!

PISTOL
With liver burning hot: prevent, or go thou,
Like Sir Actaeon he, with Ringwood at thy heels. —
O! odious is the name!

FORD
What name, sir?

PISTOL
The horn, I say. Farewell:
Take heed; have open eye, for thieves do foot by night;
Take heed, ere summer comes, or cuckoo birds do sing.
Away, Sir Corporal Nym.
Believe it, Page; he speaks sense.

[Exit PISTOL.]

FORD
[Aside] I will be patient: I will find out this.

NYM
[To PAGE] And this is true; I like not the humour of lying. He hath
wronged me in some humours: I should have borne the humoured letter
to her; but I have a sword, and it shall bite upon my necessity. He loves
your wife; there's the short and the long. My name is Corporal Nym; I
speak, and I avouch 'tis true. My name is Nym, and Falstaff loves your
wife. Adieu. I love not the humour of bread and cheese; and there's the
humour of it. Adieu.

[Exit NYM.]

PAGE
[Aside] "The humour of it," quoth 'a! Here's a fellow frights English out
of his wits.

FORD
I will seek out Falstaff.

PAGE
I never heard such a drawling, affecting rogue.

FORD
If I do find it: well.

PAGE
I will not believe such a Cataian, though the priest o' the town com-
mended him for a true man.

FORD
'Twas a good sensible fellow: well.

PAGE
How now, Meg!

[MISTRESS PAGE and MISTRESS FORD come forward.]

MRS. PAGE
Whither go you, George? — Hark you.

MRS. FORD
How now, sweet Frank! why art thou melancholy?

FORD
I melancholy! I am not melancholy. Get you home, go.

MRS. FORD
Faith, thou hast some crotchets in thy head now. Will you go, Mistress
Page?

MRS. PAGE
Have with you. You›ll come to dinner, George?
[Aside to MRS. FORD] Look who comes yonder: she shall be our messen-
ger to this paltry knight.

MRS. FORD
[Aside to MRS. PAGE] Trust me, I thought on her: she'll fit it.

[Enter MISTRESS QUICKLY.]

MRS. PAGE
You are come to see my daughter Anne?

QUICKLY
Ay, forsooth; and, I pray, how does good Mistress Anne?

MRS. PAGE
Go in with us and see; we'd have an hour's talk with you.

[Exeunt MISTRESS PAGE, MISTRESS FORD, and MISTRESS QUICKLY.]

PAGE
How now, Master Ford!

FORD
You heard what this knave told me, did you not?

PAGE
Yes; and you heard what the other told me?

FORD
Do you think there is truth in them?

PAGE
Hang 'em, slaves! I do not think the knight would offer it; but these that accuse him in his intent towards our wives are a yoke of his discarded men; very rogues, now they be out of service.

FORD
Were they his men?

PAGE
Marry, were they.

FORD
I like it never the better for that. Does he lie at the Garter?

PAGE
Ay, marry, does he. If he should intend this voyage toward my wife, I would turn her loose to him; and what he gets more of her than sharp words, let it lie on my head.

FORD
I do not misdoubt my wife; but I would be loath to turn them together. A man may be too confident. I would have nothing "lie on my head": I cannot be thus satisfied.

PAGE
Look where my ranting host of the Garter comes. There is either liquor in his pate or money in his purse when he looks so merrily.

[Enter HOST and SHALLOW.]

How now, mine host!

HOST
How now, bully-rook! Thou'rt a gentleman. Cavaliero-justice, I say!

SHALLOW
I follow, mine host, I follow. Good even and twenty, good Master Page!
Master Page, will you go with us? We have sport in hand.

HOST
Tell him, cavaliero-justice; tell him, bully-rook.

SHALLOW
Sir, there is a fray to be fought between Sir Hugh the Welsh priest and
Caius the French doctor.

FORD
Good mine host o' the Garter, a word with you.

HOST
What say'st thou, my bully-rook?

[They go aside.]

SHALLOW
[To PAGE] Will you go with us to behold it? My merry host hath had the
measuring of their weapons; and, I think, hath appointed them contrary
places; for, believe me, I hear the parson is no jester. Hark, I will tell you
what our sport shall be.

[They converse apart.]

HOST
Hast thou no suit against my knight, my guest-cavaliero?

FORD
None, I protest: but I'll give you a pottle of burnt sack to give me re-
course to him, and tell him my name is Brook, only for a jest.

HOST
My hand, bully; thou shalt have egress and regress; said I well? and thy
name shall be Brook. It is a merry knight. Will you go, mynheers?

SHALLOW
Have with you, mine host.

PAGE
I have heard the Frenchman hath good skill in his rapier.

SHALLOW

Tut, sir! I could have told you more. In these times you stand on distance, your passes, stoccadoes, and I know not what: 'tis the heart, Master Page; 'tis here, 'tis here. I have seen the time with my long sword I would have made you four tall fellows skip like rats.

HOST
Here, boys, here, here! Shall we wag?

PAGE
Have with you. I had rather hear them scold than fight.

[Exeunt HOST, SHALLOW, and PAGE.]

FORD
Though Page be a secure fool, and stands so firmly on his wife's frailty, yet I cannot put off my opinion so easily. She was in his company at Page's house, and what they made there I know not. Well, I will look further into 't; and I have a disguise to sound Falstaff. If I find her honest, I lose not my labour; if she be otherwise, 'tis labour well bestowed.

[Exit.]

SCENE II.

A ROOM IN THE GARTER INN

[Enter FALSTAFF and PISTOL.]

FALSTAFF
I will not lend thee a penny.

PISTOL
Why then, the world's mine oyster,
Which I with sword will open.
I will retort the sum in equipage.

FALSTAFF
Not a penny. I have been content, sir, you should lay my countenance to
pawn; I have grated upon my good friends for three reprieves for you
and your coach-fellow, Nym; or else you had looked through the grate,
like a geminy of baboons. I am damned in hell for swearing to gentlemen
my friends you were good soldiers and tall fellows; and when Mistress
Bridget lost the handle of her fan, I took 't upon mine honour thou hadst
it not.

PISTOL
Didst not thou share? Hadst thou not fifteen pence?

FALSTAFF
Reason, you rogue, reason. Thinkest thou I'll endanger my soul gratis?
At a word, hang no more about me, I am no gibbet for you: go: a short
knife and a throng! — to your manor of Picht-hatch! go. You'll not bear a
letter for me, you rogue! — you stand upon your honour! — Why, thou
unconfinable baseness, it is as much as I can do to keep the terms of my
honour precise. I, I, I myself sometimes, leaving the fear of God on the
left hand, and hiding mine honour in my necessity, am fain to shuffle, to
hedge, and to lurch; and yet you, rogue, will ensconce your rags, your
cat-a-mountain looks, your red-lattice phrases, and your bold-beating
oaths, under the shelter of your honour! You will not do it, you!

PISTOL
I do relent; what wouldst thou more of man?

[Enter ROBIN.]

ROBIN
Sir, here's a woman would speak with you.

FALSTAFF
Let her approach.

[Enter MISTRESS QUICKLY.]

QUICKLY
Give your worship good morrow.

FALSTAFF
Good morrow, good wife.

QUICKLY
Not so, an't please your worship.

FALSTAFF
Good maid, then.

QUICKLY
I'll be sworn;
As my mother was, the first hour I was born.

FALSTAFF
I do believe the swearer. What with me?

QUICKLY
Shall I vouchsafe your worship a word or two?

FALSTAFF
Two thousand, fair woman; and I'll vouchsafe thee the hearing.

QUICKLY
There is one Mistress Ford, sir, — I pray, come a little nearer this
ways: — I myself dwell with Master Doctor Caius.

FALSTAFF
Well, on: Mistress Ford, you say, —

QUICKLY
Your worship says very true; — I pray your worship come a little nearer
this ways.

FALSTAFF
I warrant thee nobody hears — mine own people, mine own people.

QUICKLY
Are they so? God bless them, and make them His servants!

FALSTAFF
Well: Mistress Ford, what of her?

QUICKLY
Why, sir, she's a good creature. Lord, Lord! your worship's a wanton!
Well, heaven forgive you, and all of us, I pray.

FALSTAFF
Mistress Ford; come, Mistress Ford —

QUICKLY
Marry, this is the short and the long of it. You have brought her into
such a canaries as 'tis wonderful: the best courtier of them all, when the
court lay at Windsor, could never have brought her to such a canary; yet
there has been knights, and lords, and gentlemen, with their coaches; I
warrant you, coach after coach, letter after letter, gift after gift; smelling
so sweetly, — all musk, and so rushling, I warrant you, in silk and gold;
and in such alligant terms; and in such wine and sugar of the best and
the fairest, that would have won any woman's heart; and I warrant you,
they could never get an eye-wink of her. I had myself twenty angels
given me this morning; but I defy all angels, in any such sort, as they say,
but in the way of honesty: and, I warrant you, they could never get her
so much as sip on a cup with the proudest of them all; and yet there has
been earls, nay, which is more, pensioners; but, I warrant you, all is one
with her.

FALSTAFF
But what says she to me? be brief, my good she-Mercury.

QUICKLY
Marry, she hath received your letter; for the which she thanks you a
thousand times; and she gives you to notify that her husband will be
absence from his house between ten and eleven.

FALSTAFF
Ten and eleven?

QUICKLY
Ay, forsooth; and then you may come and see the picture, she says, that
you wot of: Master Ford, her husband, will be from home. Alas! the
sweet woman leads an ill life with him; he's a very jealousy man; she
leads a very frampold life with him, good heart.

FALSTAFF
Ten and eleven. Woman, commend me to her; I will not fail her.

QUICKLY
Why, you say well. But I have another messenger to your worship:
Mistress Page hath her hearty commendations to you too; and let me tell
you in your ear, she's as fartuous a civil modest wife, and one, I tell you,
that will not miss you morning nor evening prayer, as any is in Windsor,
whoe'er be the other; and she bade me tell your worship that her husband is seldom from home, but she hopes there will come a time. I never
knew a woman so dote upon a man: surely I think you have charms, la!
yes, in truth.

FALSTAFF
Not I, I assure thee; setting the attraction of my good parts aside, I have
no other charms.

QUICKLY
Blessing on your heart for 't!

FALSTAFF
But, I pray thee, tell me this: has Ford's wife and Page's wife acquainted
each other how they love me?

QUICKLY
That were a jest indeed! They have not so little grace, I hope: that were a
trick indeed! But Mistress Page would desire you to send her your little
page, of all loves: her husband has a marvellous infection to the little
page; and, truly, Master Page is an honest man. Never a wife in Windsor
leads a better life than she does; do what she will, say what she will, take
all, pay all, go to bed when she list, rise when she list, all is as she will;
and truly she deserves it; for if there be a kind woman in Windsor, she is
one. You must send her your page; no remedy.

FALSTAFF
Why, I will.

QUICKLY
Nay, but do so then; and, look you, he may come and go between you
both; and in any case have a nay-word, that you may know one another's
mind, and the boy never need to understand any thing; for 'tis not good
that children should know any wickedness: old folks, you know, have
discretion, as they say, and know the world.

FALSTAFF

Fare thee well; commend me to them both. There's my purse; I am yet thy debtor. Boy, go along with this woman. —

[Exeunt MISTRESS QUICKLY and ROBIN.]

This news distracts me.

PISTOL
This punk is one of Cupid's carriers;
Clap on more sails; pursue; up with your fights;
Give fire; she is my prize, or ocean whelm them all!

[Exit PISTOL.]

FALSTAFF
Say'st thou so, old Jack? go thy ways; I'll make more of thy old body than I have done. Will they yet look after thee? Wilt thou, after the expense of so much money, be now a gainer? Good body, I thank thee. Let them say 'tis grossly done; so it be fairly done, no matter.

[Enter BARDOLPH, with a cup of sack.]

BARDOLPH
Sir John, there's one Master Brook below would fain speak with you and be acquainted with you: and hath sent your worship a morning's draught of sack.

FALSTAFF
Brook is his name?

BARDOLPH
Ay, sir.

FALSTAFF
Call him in.

[Exit BARDOLPH.]

Such Brooks are welcome to me, that o'erflow such liquor. Ah, ha! Mistress Ford and Mistress Page, have I encompassed you? Go to; via!

[Re-enter BARDOLPH, with FORD disguised.]

FORD
Bless you, sir!

FALSTAFF
And you, sir; would you speak with me?

FORD
I make bold to press with so little preparation upon you.

FALSTAFF

You're welcome. What's your will? — Give us leave, drawer.

[Exit BARDOLPH.]

FORD
Sir, I am a gentleman that have spent much: my name is Brook.

FALSTAFF
Good Master Brook, I desire more acquaintance of you.

FORD
Good Sir John, I sue for yours: not to charge you; for I must let you understand I think myself in better plight for a lender than you are: the which hath something embold'ned me to this unseasoned intrusion; for they say, if money go before, all ways do lie open.

FALSTAFF
Money is a good soldier, sir, and will on.

FORD
Troth, and I have a bag of money here troubles me; if you will help to bear it, Sir John, take all, or half, for easing me of the carriage.

FALSTAFF
Sir, I know not how I may deserve to be your porter.

FORD
I will tell you, sir, if you will give me the hearing.

FALSTAFF
Speak, good Master Brook; I shall be glad to be your servant.

FORD
Sir, I hear you are a scholar, — I will be brief with you, and you have been a man long known to me, though I had never so good means, as desire, to make myself acquainted with you. I shall discover a thing to you, wherein I must very much lay open mine own imperfection; but, good Sir John, as you have one eye upon my follies, as you hear them un-folded, turn another into the register of your own, that I may pass with a reproof the easier, sith you yourself know how easy is it to be such an offender.

FALSTAFF
Very well, sir; proceed.

FORD
There is a gentlewoman in this town, her husband's name is Ford.

FALSTAFF
Well, sir.

FORD
I have long loved her, and, I protest to you, bestowed much on her;
followed her with a doting observance; engrossed opportunities to meet
her; fee'd every slight occasion that could but niggardly give me sight of
her; not only bought many presents to give her, but have given largely
to many to know what she would have given; briefly, I have pursued her
as love hath pursued me; which hath been on the wing of all occasions.
But whatsoever I have merited, either in my mind or in my means, meed,
I am sure, I have received none, unless experience be a jewel that I have
purchased at an infinite rate, and that hath taught me to say this,

Love like a shadow flies when substance love pursues;
Pursuing that that flies, and flying what pursues.

FALSTAFF
Have you received no promise of satisfaction at her hands?

FORD
Never.

FALSTAFF
Have you importuned her to such a purpose?

FORD
Never.

FALSTAFF
Of what quality was your love, then?

FORD
Like a fair house built on another man's ground; so that I have lost my
edifice by mistaking the place where I erected it.

FALSTAFF
To what purpose have you unfolded this to me?

FORD
When I have told you that, I have told you all. Some say that though she
appear honest to me, yet in other places she enlargeth her mirth so far
that there is shrewd construction made of her. Now, Sir John, here is the
heart of my purpose: you are a gentleman of excellent breeding, admirable discourse, of great admittance, authentic in your place and person,
generally allowed for your many war-like, court-like, and learnèd prepa-

rations.

FALSTAFF
O, sir!

FORD
Believe it, for you know it. There is money; spend it, spend it; spend
more; spend all I have; only give me so much of your time in exchange
of it as to lay an amiable siege to the honesty of this Ford's wife: use your
art of wooing, win her to consent to you; if any man may, you may as
soon as any.

FALSTAFF
Would it apply well to the vehemency of your affection, that I should
win what you would enjoy? Methinks you prescribe to yourself very
preposterously.

FORD
O, understand my drift. She dwells so securely on the excellency of her
honour that the folly of my soul dares not present itself; she is too bright
to be looked against. Now, could I come to her with any detection in my
hand, my desires had instance and argument to commend themselves;
I could drive her then from the ward of her purity, her reputation, her
marriage-vow, and a thousand other her defences, which now are too too
strongly embattled against me. What say you to't, Sir John?

FALSTAFF
Master Brook, I will first make bold with your money; next, give me your
hand; and last, as I am a gentleman, you shall, if you will, enjoy Ford's
wife.

FORD
O good sir!

FALSTAFF
I say you shall.

FORD
Want no money, Sir John; you shall want none.

FALSTAFF
Want no Mistress Ford, Master Brook; you shall want none. I shall be
with her, I may tell you, by her own appointment; even as you came in to
me her assistant or go-between parted from me: I say I shall be with her
between ten and eleven; for at that time the jealous rascally knave, her
husband, will be forth. Come you to me at night; you shall know how I

speed.

FORD
I am blest in your acquaintance. Do you know Ford, sir?

FALSTAFF
Hang him, poor cuckoldly knave! I know him not; yet I wrong him to call him poor; they say the jealous wittolly knave hath masses of money; for the which his wife seems to me well-favoured. I will use her as the key of the cuckoldly rogue's coffer; and there's my harvest-home.

FORD
I would you knew Ford, sir, that you might avoid him if you saw him.

FALSTAFF
Hang him, mechanical salt-butter rogue! I will stare him out of his wits; I will awe him with my cudgel; it shall hang like a meteor o'er the cuckold's horns. Master Brook, thou shalt know I will predominate over the peasant, and thou shalt lie with his wife. Come to me soon at night. Ford's a knave, and I will aggravate his style; thou, Master Brook, shalt know him for knave and cuckold. Come to me soon at night.

[Exit FALSTAFF.]

FORD
What a damned Epicurean rascal is this! My heart is ready to crack with impatience. Who says this is improvident jealousy? My wife hath sent to him; the hour is fixed; the match is made. Would any man have thought this? See the hell of having a false woman! My bed shall be abused, my coffers ransacked, my reputation gnawn at; and I shall not only receive this villanous wrong, but stand under the adoption of abominable terms, and by him that does me this wrong. Terms! names! Amaimon sounds well; Lucifer, well; Barbason, well; yet they are devils' additions, the names of fiends. But Cuckold! Wittol! — Cuckold! the devil himself hath not such a name. Page is an ass, a secure ass; he will trust his wife; he will not be jealous; I will rather trust a Fleming with my butter, Parson Hugh the Welshman with my cheese, an Irishman with my aqua-vitae bottle, or a thief to walk my ambling gelding, than my wife with herself; then she plots, then she ruminates, then she devises; and what they think in their hearts they may effect, they will break their hearts but they will effect. God be praised for my jealousy! Eleven o'clock the hour. I will prevent this, detect my wife, be revenged on Falstaff, and laugh at Page. I will about it; better three hours too soon than a minute too late. Fie, fie, fie! cuckold! cuckold! cuckold!

[Exit.]

SCENE III.

A FIELD NEAR WINDSOR

[Enter CAIUS and RUGBY.]

CAIUS
Jack Rugby!

RUGBY
Sir?

CAIUS
Vat is de clock, Jack?

RUGBY
'Tis past the hour, sir, that Sir Hugh promised to meet.

CAIUS
By gar, he has save his soul, dat he is no come; he has pray his Pible vell dat he is no come: by gar, Jack Rugby, he is dead already, if he be come.

RUGBY
He is wise, sir; he knew your worship would kill him if he came.

CAIUS
By gar, de herring is no dead so as I vill kill him. Take your rapier, Jack; I vill tell you how I vill kill him.

RUGBY
Alas, sir, I cannot fence!

CAIUS
Villany, take your rapier.

RUGBY
Forbear; here's company.

[Enter HOST, SHALLOW, SLENDER, and PAGE.]

HOST

Bless thee, bully doctor!

SHALLOW
Save you, Master Doctor Caius!

PAGE
Now, good Master Doctor!

SLENDER
Give you good morrow, sir.

CAIUS
Vat be all you, one, two, tree, four, come for?

HOST
To see thee fight, to see thee foin, to see thee traverse; to see thee here, to
see thee there; to see thee pass thy punto, thy stock, thy reverse, thy distance, thy montant. Is he dead, my Ethiopian? Is he dead, my Francisco?
Ha, bully! What says my Aesculapius? my Galen? my heart of elder? Ha!
is he dead, bully stale? Is he dead?

CAIUS
By gar, he is de coward Jack priest of de world; he is not show his face.

HOST
Thou art a Castalion King Urinal! Hector of Greece, my boy!

CAIUS
I pray you, bear witness that me have stay six or seven, two, tree hours
for him, and he is no come.

SHALLOW
He is the wiser man, Master doctor: he is a curer of souls, and you a curer of bodies; if you should fight, you go against the hair of your profes-
sions. Is it not true, Master Page?

PAGE
Master Shallow, you have yourself been a great fighter, though now a
man of peace.

SHALLOW
Bodykins, Master Page, though I now be old, and of the peace, if I see
a sword out, my finger itches to make one. Though we are justices, and
doctors, and churchmen, Master Page, we have some salt of our youth in
us; we are the sons of women, Master Page.

PAGE
'Tis true, Master Shallow.

SHALLOW
It will be found so, Master Page. Master Doctor Caius, I come to fetch
you home. I am sworn of the peace; you have showed yourself a wise
physician, and Sir Hugh hath shown himself a wise and patient church-
man. You must go with me, Master Doctor.

HOST
Pardon, guest-justice. — A word, Monsieur Mockwater.

CAIUS
Mock-vater! Vat is dat?

HOST
Mockwater, in our English tongue, is valour, bully.

CAIUS
By gar, then I have as much mockvater as de Englishman. — Scurvy jack-
dog priest! By gar, me vill cut his ears.

HOST
He will clapper-claw thee tightly, bully.

CAIUS
Clapper-de-claw! Vat is dat?

HOST
That is, he will make thee amends.

CAIUS
By gar, me do look he shall clapper-de-claw me; for, by gar, me vill have
it.

HOST
And I will provoke him to't, or let him wag.

CAIUS
Me tank you for dat.

HOST
And, moreover, bully — but first: Master guest, and Master Page, and
eke Cavaliero Slender, go you through the town to Frogmore.

[Aside to them]

PAGE
Sir Hugh is there, is he?

HOST
He is there: see what humour he is in; and I will bring the doctor about by the fields. Will it do well?

SHALLOW
We will do it.

PAGE, SHALLOW, and SLENDER
Adieu, good Master Doctor.

[Exeunt PAGE, SHALLOW, and SLENDER.]

CAIUS
By gar, me vill kill de priest; for he speak for a jack-an-ape to Anne Page.

HOST
Let him die. Sheathe thy impatience; throw cold water on thy choler; go about the fields with me through Frogmore; I will bring thee where Mistress Anne Page is, at a farm-house a-feasting; and thou shalt woo her. Cried I aim! Said I well?

CAIUS
By gar, me tank you for dat: by gar, I love you; and I shall procure-a you de good guest, de earl, de knight, de lords, de gentlemen, my patients.

HOST
For the which I will be thy adversary toward Anne Page: said I well?

CAIUS
By gar, 'tis good; vell said.

HOST
Let us wag, then.

CAIUS
Come at my heels, Jack Rugby.

[Exeunt.]

ACT III

SCENE I.

A FIELD NEAR FROGMORE

[Enter SIR HUGH EVANS and SIMPLE.]

EVANS
I pray you now, good Master Slender's serving-man, and friend Simple by your name, which way have you looked for Master Caius, that calls himself doctor of physic?

SIMPLE
Marry, sir, the pittie-ward, the park-ward, every way; old Windsor way, and every way but the town way.

EVANS
I most fehemently desire you you will also look that way.

SIMPLE
I will, Sir.

[Exit SIMPLE.]

EVANS
Pless my soul, how full of chollors I am, and trempling of mind! I shall be glad if he have deceived me. How melancholies I am! I will knog his urinals about his knave's costard when I have goot opportunities for the 'ork: pless my soul!

[Sings]

To shallow rivers, to whose falls
Melodious birds sings madrigals;
There will we make our peds of roses,
And a thousand fragrant posies.
To shallow —

Mercy on me! I have a great dispositions to cry.

[Sings]

Melodious birds sing madrigals, —
Whenas I sat in Pabylon, —

And a thousand vagram posies.
To shallow, —

[Re-enter SIMPLE.]

SIMPLE
Yonder he is, coming this way, Sir Hugh.

EVANS
He's welcome.

[Sings]

To shallow rivers, to whose falls —

Heaven prosper the right! — What weapons is he?

SIMPLE
No weapons, sir. There comes my master, Master Shallow, and another gentleman, from Frogmore, over the stile, this way.

EVANS
Pray you give me my gown; or else keep it in your arms. *[Reads in a book.]*

[Enter PAGE, SHALLOW, and SLENDER.]

SHALLOW
How now, Master Parson! Good morrow, good Sir Hugh. Keep a gamester from the dice, and a good student from his book, and it is wonderful.

SLENDER
[Aside] Ah, sweet Anne Page!

PAGE
'Save you, good Sir Hugh!

EVANS
Pless you from his mercy sake, all of you!

SHALLOW
What, the sword and the word! Do you study them both, Master Parson?

PAGE
And youthful still, in your doublet and hose, this raw rheumatic day!

EVANS
There is reasons and causes for it.

PAGE
We are come to you to do a good office, Master Parson.

EVANS
Fery well; what is it?

PAGE
Yonder is a most reverend gentleman, who, belike having received
wrong by some person, is at most odds with his own gravity and patience that ever you saw.

SHALLOW
I have lived fourscore years and upward; I never heard a man of his
place, gravity, and learning, so wide of his own respect.

EVANS
What is he?

PAGE
I think you know him: Master Doctor Caius, the renowned French physician.

EVANS
Got's will and His passion of my heart! I had as lief you would tell me of
a mess of porridge.

PAGE
Why?

EVANS
He has no more knowledge in Hibbocrates and Galen, — and he is a
knave besides; a cowardly knave as you would desires to be acquainted
withal.

PAGE
I warrant you, he's the man should fight with him.

SLENDER
[Aside] O, sweet Anne Page!

SHALLOW
It appears so, by his weapons. Keep them asunder; here comes Doctor
Caius.

[Enter HOST, CAIUS, and RUGBY.]

PAGE
Nay, good Master Parson, keep in your weapon.

SHALLOW
So do you, good Master Doctor.

HOST
Disarm them, and let them question; let them keep their limbs whole and hack our English.

CAIUS
I pray you, let-a me speak a word with your ear: verefore will you not meet-a me?

EVANS
[Aside to CAIUS] Pray you use your patience; in good time.

CAIUS
By gar, you are de coward, de Jack dog, John ape.

EVANS
[Aside to CAIUS] Pray you, let us not be laughing-stogs to other men's humours; I desire you in friendship, and I will one way or other make you amends.
[Aloud] I will knog your urinals about your knave's cogscomb for missing your meetings and appointments.

CAIUS
Diable! — Jack Rugby, — mine Host de Jarretiere, — have I not stay for him to kill him? Have I not, at de place I did appoint?

EVANS
As I am a Christians soul, now, look you, this is the place appointed. I'll be judgment by mine host of the Garter.

HOST
Peace, I say, Gallia and Gaullia; French and Welsh, soul-curer and body-curer!

CAIUS
Ay, dat is very good; excellent!

HOST
Peace, I say! Hear mine host of the Garter. Am I politic? am I subtle? am I a Machiavel? Shall I lose my doctor? No; he gives me the potions and the motions. Shall I lose my parson, my priest, my Sir Hugh? No; he gives me the proverbs and the no-verbs. Give me thy hand, terrestrial; so; — give me thy hand, celestial; so. Boys of art, I have deceived you both; I have directed you to wrong places; your hearts are mighty, your

skins are whole, and let burnt sack be the issue. Come, lay their swords to pawn. Follow me, lads of peace; follow, follow, follow.

SHALLOW
Trust me, a mad host! — Follow, gentlemen, follow.

SLENDER
[Aside] O, sweet Anne Page!

[Exeunt SHALLOW, SLENDER, PAGE, and HOST.]

CAIUS
Ha, do I perceive dat? Have you make-a de sot of us, ha, ha?

EVANS
This is well; he has made us his vlouting-stog. I desire you that we may be friends; and let us knog our prains together to be revenge on this same scall, scurvy, cogging companion, the host of the Garter.

CAIUS
By gar, with all my heart. He promise to bring me where is Anne Page; by gar, he deceive me too.

EVANS
Well, I will smite his noddles. Pray you follow.

[Exeunt.]

SCENE II.

A STREET IN WINDSOR

[Enter MISTRESS PAGE and ROBIN.]

MRS. PAGE
Nay, keep your way, little gallant: you were wont to be a follower, but now you are a leader. Whether had you rather lead mine eyes, or eye your master's heels?

ROBIN
I had rather, forsooth, go before you like a man than follow him like a dwarf.

MRS. PAGE
O! you are a flattering boy: now I see you'll be a courtier.

[Enter FORD.]

FORD
Well met, Mistress Page. Whither go you?

MRS. PAGE
Truly, sir, to see your wife. Is she at home?

FORD
Ay; and as idle as she may hang together, for want of company. I think, if your husbands were dead, you two would marry.

MRS. PAGE
Be sure of that — two other husbands.

FORD
Where had you this pretty weathercock?

MRS. PAGE
I cannot tell what the dickens his name is my husband had him of. What do you call your knight's name, sirrah?

ROBIN

Sir John Falstaff.

FORD
Sir John Falstaff!

MRS. PAGE
He, he; I can never hit on's name. There is such a league between my
good man and he! Is your wife at home indeed?

FORD
Indeed she is.

MRS. PAGE
By your leave, sir: I am sick till I see her.

[Exeunt MRS. PAGE and ROBIN.]

FORD
Has Page any brains? Hath he any eyes? Hath he any thinking? Sure,
they sleep; he hath no use of them. Why, this boy will carry a letter twenty mile as easy as a cannon will shoot point-blank twelve score. He pieces
out his wife's inclination; he gives her folly motion and advantage; and
now she's going to my wife, and Falstaff's boy with her. A man may hear
this shower sing in the wind: and Falstaff's boy with her! Good plots!
They are laid; and our revolted wives share damnation together. Well; I
will take him, then torture my wife, pluck the borrowed veil of modesty
from the so seeming Mistress Page, divulge Page himself for a secure and
wilful Actaeon; and to these violent proceedings all my neighbours shall
cry aim. *[Clock strikes.]* The clock gives me my cue, and my assurance
bids me search; there I shall find Falstaff. I shall be rather praised for this
than mocked; for it is as positive as the earth is firm that Falstaff is there.
I will go.

*[Enter PAGE, SHALLOW, SLENDER, HOST, SIR HUGH EVANS, CAIUS,
and RUGBY.]*

SHALLOW, PAGE, &c
Well met, Master Ford.

FORD
Trust me, a good knot; I have good cheer at home, and I pray you all go
with me.

SHALLOW
I must excuse myself, Master Ford.

SLENDER
And so must I, sir; we have appointed to dine with Mistress Anne, and I
would not break with her for more money than I'll speak of.

SHALLOW
We have lingered about a match between Anne Page and my cousin Slender, and this day we shall have our answer.

SLENDER
I hope I have your good will, father Page.

PAGE
You have, Master Slender; I stand wholly for you. But my wife, Master doctor, is for you altogether.

CAIUS
Ay, be-gar; and de maid is love-a me: my nursh-a Quickly tell me so mush.

HOST
What say you to young Master Fenton? He capers, he dances, he has eyes of youth, he writes verses, he speaks holiday, he smells April and May; he will carry 't, he will carry 't; 'tis in his buttons; he will carry 't.

PAGE
Not by my consent, I promise you. The gentleman is of no having: he kept company with the wild Prince and Pointz; he is of too high a region, he knows too much. No, he shall not knit a knot in his fortunes with the finger of my substance; if he take her, let him take her simply; the wealth I have waits on my consent, and my consent goes not that way.

FORD
I beseech you, heartily, some of you go home with me to dinner: besides your cheer, you shall have sport; I will show you a monster. Master Doctor, you shall go; so shall you, Master Page; and you, Sir Hugh.

SHALLOW
Well, fare you well; we shall have the freer wooing at Master Page's.

[Exeunt SHALLOW and SLENDER.]

CAIUS
Go home, John Rugby; I come anon.

[Exit RUGBY.]

HOST
Farewell, my hearts; I will to my honest knight Falstaff, and drink canary with him.

[Exit HOST.]

FORD

[Aside] I think I shall drink in pipe-wine first with him. I'll make him dance.
Will you go, gentles?

ALL
Have with you to see this monster.

[Exeunt.]

SCENE III.

A ROOM IN FORD'S HOUSE

[Enter MISTRESS FORD and MISTRESS PAGE.]

MRS. FORD
What, John! what, Robert!

MRS. PAGE
Quickly, quickly: — Is the buck-basket —

MRS. FORD
I warrant. What, Robin, I say!

[Enter SERVANTS with a basket.]

MRS. PAGE
Come, come, come.

MRS. FORD
Here, set it down.

MRS. PAGE
Give your men the charge; we must be brief.

MRS. FORD
Marry, as I told you before, John and Robert, be ready here hard by in the brew-house; and when I suddenly call you, come forth, and, without any pause or staggering, take this basket on your shoulders: that done, trudge with it in all haste, and carry it among the whitsters in Datchet-Mead, and there empty it in the muddy ditch close by the Thames side.

MRS. PAGE
You will do it?

MRS. FORD
I have told them over and over; they lack no direction. Be gone, and come when you are called.

[Exeunt SERVANTS.]

MRS. PAGE
Here comes little Robin.

[Enter ROBIN.]

MRS. FORD
How now, my eyas-musket! what news with you?

ROBIN
My Master Sir John is come in at your back-door, Mistress Ford, and requests your company.

MRS. PAGE
You little Jack-a-Lent, have you been true to us?

ROBIN
Ay, I'll be sworn. My master knows not of your being here, and hath threatened to put me into everlasting liberty, if I tell you of it; for he swears he'll turn me away.

MRS. PAGE
Thou 'rt a good boy; this secrecy of thine shall be a tailor to thee, and shall make thee a new doublet and hose. I'll go hide me.

MRS. FORD
Do so. Go tell thy master I am alone.

[Exit ROBIN.]

Mistress Page, remember you your cue.

MRS. PAGE
I warrant thee; if I do not act it, hiss me.

[Exit MISTRESS PAGE.]

MRS. FORD
Go to, then; we'll use this unwholesome humidity, this gross watery pumpion; we'll teach him to know turtles from jays.

[Enter FALSTAFF.]

FALSTAFF
"Have I caught thee, my heavenly jewel?" Why, now let me die, for I have lived long enough: this is the period of my ambition: O this blessed hour!

MRS. FORD
O, sweet Sir John!

FALSTAFF

Mistress Ford, I cannot cog, I cannot prate, Mistress Ford. Now shall I sin in my wish; I would thy husband were dead. I'll speak it before the best lord, I would make thee my lady.

MRS. FORD
I your lady, Sir John! Alas, I should be a pitiful lady.

FALSTAFF
Let the court of France show me such another. I see how thine eye would emulate the diamond; thou hast the right arched beauty of the brow that becomes the ship-tire, the tire-valiant, or any tire of Venetian admittance.

MRS. FORD
A plain kerchief, Sir John; my brows become nothing else; nor that well neither.

FALSTAFF
By the Lord, thou art a traitor to say so: thou wouldst make an absolute courtier; and the firm fixture of thy foot would give an excellent motion to thy gait in a semi-circled farthingale. I see what thou wert, if Fortune thy foe were not, Nature thy friend. Come, thou canst not hide it.

MRS. FORD
Believe me, there's no such thing in me.

FALSTAFF
What made me love thee? Let that persuade thee there's something extraordinary in thee. Come, I cannot cog and say thou art this and that, like a many of these lisping hawthorn-buds that come like women in men's apparel, and smell like Bucklersbury in simple-time; I cannot; but I love thee, none but thee; and thou deservest it.

MRS. FORD
Do not betray me, sir; I fear you love Mistress Page.

FALSTAFF
Thou mightst as well say I love to walk by the Counter-gate, which is as hateful to me as the reek of a lime-kiln.

MRS. FORD
Well, heaven knows how I love you; and you shall one day find it.

FALSTAFF
Keep in that mind; I'll deserve it.

MRS. FORD

Nay, I must tell you, so you do; or else I could not be in that mind.

ROBIN
[Within] Mistress Ford! Mistress Ford! here's Mistress Page at the door, sweating and blowing and looking wildly, and would needs speak with you presently.

FALSTAFF
She shall not see me; I will ensconce me behind the arras.

MRS. FORD
Pray you, do so; she's a very tattling woman.
[FALSTAFF hides himself.]

[Re-enter MISTRESS PAGE and ROBIN.]
What's the matter? How now!

MRS. PAGE
O Mistress Ford, what have you done? You're shamed, you are overthrown, you are undone for ever!

MRS. FORD
What's the matter, good Mistress Page?

MRS. PAGE
O well-a-day, Mistress Ford! having an honest man to your husband, to give him such cause of suspicion!

MRS. FORD
What cause of suspicion?

MRS. PAGE
What cause of suspicion? Out upon you! how am I mistook in you!

MRS. FORD
Why, alas, what's the matter?

MRS. PAGE
Your husband's coming hither, woman, with all the officers in Windsor, to search for a gentleman that he says is here now in the house, by your consent, to take an ill advantage of his absence: you are undone.

MRS. FORD
[Aside] Speak louder.

'Tis not so, I hope.

MRS. PAGE
Pray heaven it be not so that you have such a man here! but 'tis most
certain your husband's coming, with half Windsor at his heels, to search
for such a one. I come before to tell you. If you know yourself clear, why,
I am glad of it; but if you have a friend here, convey, convey him out. Be
not amazed; call all your senses to you; defend your reputation, or bid
farewell to your good life for ever.

MRS. FORD
What shall I do? — There is a gentleman, my dear friend; and I fear
not mine own shame as much as his peril: I had rather than a thousand
pound he were out of the house.

MRS. PAGE
For shame! never stand "you had rather" and "you had rather": your
husband's here at hand; bethink you of some conveyance; in the house
you cannot hide him. O, how have you deceived me! Look, here is a
basket; if he be of any reasonable stature, he may creep in here; and
throw foul linen upon him, as if it were going to bucking: or — it is whit-
ing-time — send him by your two men to Datchet-Mead.

MRS. FORD
He's too big to go in there. What shall I do?

FALSTAFF
[Coming forward] Let me see 't, let me see 't. O, let me see 't! I'll in, I'll in;
follow your friend's counsel; I'll in.

MRS. PAGE
What, Sir John Falstaff! Are these your letters, knight?

FALSTAFF
I love thee and none but thee; help me away: let me creep in here. I'll
never —

[He gets into the basket; they cover him with foul linen.]

MRS. PAGE
Help to cover your master, boy. Call your men, Mistress Ford. You dis-
sembling knight!

MRS. FORD
What, John! Robert! John!

[Exit ROBIN.]

[Re-enter SERVANTS.]

Go, take up these clothes here, quickly; where's the cowl-staff? Look how you drumble! Carry them to the laundress in Datchet-Mead; quickly, come.

[Enter FORD, PAGE, CAIUS, and SIR HUGH EVANS.]

FORD
Pray you come near. If I suspect without cause, why then make sport at me, then let me be your jest; I deserve it. How now, whither bear you this?

SERVANT
To the laundress, forsooth.

MRS. FORD
Why, what have you to do whither they bear it? You were best meddle with buck-washing.

FORD
Buck! I would I could wash myself of the buck! Buck, buck, buck! ay, buck; I warrant you, buck; and of the season too, it shall appear.

[Exeunt SERVANTS with the basket.]

Gentlemen, I have dreamed to-night; I'll tell you my dream. Here, here, here be my keys: ascend my chambers; search, seek, find out. I'll warrant we'll unkennel the fox. Let me stop this way first. *[Locking the door]* So, now uncape.

PAGE
Good Master Ford, be contented: you wrong yourself too much.

FORD
True, Master Page. Up, gentlemen, you shall see sport anon; follow me, gentlemen.

[Exit FORD.]

EVANS
This is fery fantastical humours and jealousies.

CAIUS
By gar, 'tis no the fashion of France; it is not jealous in France.

PAGE
Nay, follow him, gentlemen; see the issue of his search.

[Exeunt EVANS, PAGE, and CAIUS.]

MRS. PAGE

Is there not a double excellency in this?

MRS. FORD
I know not which pleases me better, that my husband is deceived, or Sir John.

MRS. PAGE
What a taking was he in when your husband asked who was in the basket!

MRS. FORD
I am half afraid he will have need of washing; so throwing him into the water will do him a benefit.

MRS. PAGE
Hang him, dishonest rascal! I would all of the same strain were in the same distress.

MRS. FORD
I think my husband hath some special suspicion of Falstaff's being here, for I never saw him so gross in his jealousy till now.

MRS. PAGE
I will lay a plot to try that, and we will yet have more tricks with Falstaff: his dissolute disease will scarce obey this medicine.

MRS. FORD
Shall we send that foolish carrion, Mistress Quickly, to him, and excuse his throwing into the water, and give him another hope, to betray him to another punishment?

MRS. PAGE
We will do it; let him be sent for to-morrow eight o'clock, to have amends.

[Re-enter FORD, PAGE, CAIUS, and SIR HUGH EVANS.]

FORD
I cannot find him: may be the knave bragged of that he could not compass.

MRS. PAGE
[Aside to MRS. FORD] Heard you that?

MRS. FORD
[Aside to MRS. PAGE] Ay, ay, peace. —
You use me well, Master Ford, do you?

FORD
Ay, I do so.

MRS. FORD
Heaven make you better than your thoughts!

FORD
Amen!

MRS. PAGE
You do yourself mighty wrong, Master Ford.

FORD
Ay, ay; I must bear it.

EVANS
If there be any pody in the house, and in the chambers, and in the coffers, and in the presses, heaven forgive my sins at the day of judgment!

CAIUS
Be gar, nor I too; there is no bodies.

PAGE
Fie, fie, Master Ford, are you not ashamed? What spirit, what devil suggests this imagination? I would not ha' your distemper in this kind for the wealth of Windsor Castle.

FORD
'Tis my fault, Master Page: I suffer for it.

EVANS
You suffer for a pad conscience. Your wife is as honest a 'omans as I will desires among five thousand, and five hundred too.

CAIUS
By gar, I see 'tis an honest woman.

FORD
Well, I promised you a dinner. Come, come, walk in the Park: I pray you pardon me; I will hereafter make known to you why I have done this. Come, wife, come, Mistress Page; I pray you pardon me; pray heartily, pardon me.

PAGE
Let's go in, gentlemen; but, trust me, we'll mock him. I do invite you

to-morrow morning to my house to breakfast; after, we'll a-birding together; I have a fine hawk for the bush. Shall it be so?

FORD
Any thing.

EVANS
If there is one, I shall make two in the company.

CAIUS
If there be one or two, I shall make-a the turd.

FORD
Pray you go, Master Page.

EVANS
I pray you now, remembrance to-morrow on the lousy knave, mine host.

CAIUS
Dat is good; by gar, with all my heart.

EVANS
A lousy knave! to have his gibes and his mockeries!

[Exeunt.]

SCENE IV.

A ROOM IN PAGE'S HOUSE

[Enter FENTON, ANNE PAGE, and MISTRESS QUICKLY. MISTRESS QUICKLY stands apart.]

FENTON
I see I cannot get thy father's love;
Therefore no more turn me to him, sweet Nan.

ANNE
Alas! how then?

FENTON
Why, thou must be thyself.
He doth object, I am too great of birth;
And that my state being gall'd with my expense,
I seek to heal it only by his wealth.
Besides these, other bars he lays before me,
My riots past, my wild societies;
And tells me 'tis a thing impossible
I should love thee but as a property.

ANNE
May be he tells you true.

FENTON
No, heaven so speed me in my time to come!
Albeit I will confess thy father's wealth
Was the first motive that I wooed thee, Anne:
Yet, wooing thee, I found thee of more value
Than stamps in gold, or sums in sealèd bags;
And 'tis the very riches of thyself
That now I aim at.

ANNE
Gentle Master Fenton,
Yet seek my father's love; still seek it, sir.
If opportunity and humblest suit

Cannot attain it, why then, — hark you hither.

[They converse apart.]

[Enter SHALLOW, SLENDER, and MISTRESS QUICKLY.]

SHALLOW
Break their talk, Mistress Quickly: my kinsman shall speak for himself.

SLENDER
I'll make a shaft or a bolt on 't. 'Slid, 'tis but venturing.

SHALLOW
Be not dismayed.

SLENDER
No, she shall not dismay me. I care not for that, but that I am afeard.

QUICKLY
Hark ye; Master Slender would speak a word with you.

ANNE
I come to him.
[Aside] This is my father›s choice.
O, what a world of vile ill-favour'd faults
Looks handsome in three hundred pounds a year!

QUICKLY
And how does good Master Fenton? Pray you, a word with you.

SHALLOW
She's coming; to her, coz. O boy, thou hadst a father!

SLENDER
I had a father, Mistress Anne; my uncle can tell you good jests of him.
Pray you, uncle, tell Mistress Anne the jest how my father stole two
geese out of a pen, good uncle.

SHALLOW
Mistress Anne, my cousin loves you.

SLENDER
Ay, that I do; as well as I love any woman in Gloucestershire.

SHALLOW
He will maintain you like a gentlewoman.

SLENDER
Ay, that I will come cut and long-tail, under the degree of a squire.

SHALLOW
He will make you a hundred and fifty pounds jointure.

ANNE
Good Master Shallow, let him woo for himself.

SHALLOW
Marry, I thank you for it; I thank you for that good comfort. She calls you, coz; I'll leave you.

ANNE
Now, Master Slender.

SLENDER
Now, good Mistress Anne. —

ANNE
What is your will?

SLENDER
My will! 'od's heartlings, that's a pretty jest indeed! I ne'er made my will yet, I thank heaven; I am not such a sickly creature, I give heaven praise.

ANNE
I mean, Master Slender, what would you with me?

SLENDER
Truly, for mine own part I would little or nothing with you. Your father and my uncle hath made motions; if it be my luck, so; if not, happy man be his dole! They can tell you how things go better than I can. You may ask your father; here he comes.

[Enter PAGE and MISTRESS PAGE.]

PAGE
Now, Master Slender: love him, daughter Anne.
Why, how now! what does Master Fenton here?
You wrong me, sir, thus still to haunt my house:
I told you, sir, my daughter is dispos'd of.

FENTON
Nay, Master Page, be not impatient.

MRS. PAGE

Good Master Fenton, come not to my child.

PAGE
She is no match for you.

FENTON
Sir, will you hear me?

PAGE
No, good Master Fenton.
Come, Master Shallow; come, son Slender, in.
Knowing my mind, you wrong me, Master Fenton.

[Exeunt PAGE, SHALLOW, and SLENDER.]

QUICKLY
Speak to Mistress Page.

FENTON
Good Mistress Page, for that I love your daughter
In such a righteous fashion as I do,
Perforce, against all checks, rebukes, and manners,
I must advance the colours of my love
And not retire: let me have your good will.

ANNE
Good mother, do not marry me to yond fool.

MRS. PAGE
I mean it not; I seek you a better husband.

QUICKLY
That's my master, Master doctor.

ANNE
Alas! I had rather be set quick i' the earth.
And bowl'd to death with turnips.

MRS. PAGE
Come, trouble not yourself. Good Master Fenton,
I will not be your friend, nor enemy;
My daughter will I question how she loves you,
And as I find her, so am I affected.
Till then, farewell, sir: she must needs go in;
Her father will be angry.

FENTON

Farewell, gentle mistress. Farewell, Nan.

[Exeunt MRS. PAGE and ANNE.]

QUICKLY
This is my doing now: "Nay," said I, "will you cast away your child on a
fool, and a physician? Look on Master Fenton." This is my doing.

FENTON
I thank thee; and I pray thee, once to-night
Give my sweet Nan this ring. There's for thy pains.

QUICKLY
Now Heaven send thee good fortune!

[Exit FENTON.]

A kind heart he hath; a woman would run through fire and water for
such a kind heart. But yet I would my master had Mistress Anne; or I
would Master Slender had her; or, in sooth, I would Master Fenton had
her; I will do what I can for them all three, for so I have promised, and I'll
be as good as my word; but speciously for Master Fenton. Well, I must of
another errand to Sir John Falstaff from my two mistresses: what a beast
am I to slack it!

[Exit.]

SCENE V.

A ROOM IN THE GARTER INN

[Enter FALSTAFF and BARDOLPH.]

FALSTAFF
Bardolph, I say, —

BARDOLPH
Here, sir.

FALSTAFF
Go fetch me a quart of sack; put a toast in 't.

[Exit BARDOLPH.]

Have I lived to be carried in a basket, and to be thrown in the Thames like a barrow of butcher's offal? Well, if I be served such another trick, I'll have my brains ta'en out and buttered, and give them to a dog for a new year's gift. The rogues slighted me into the river with as little remorse as they would have drowned a blind bitch's puppies, fifteen i' the litter; and you may know by my size that I have a kind of alacrity in sinking; if the bottom were as deep as hell I should down. I had been drowned but that the shore was shelvy and shallow; a death that I abhor, for the water swells a man; and what a thing should I have been when had been swelled! I should have been a mountain of mummy.

[Re-enter BARDOLPH, with the sack.]

BARDOLPH
Here's Mistress Quickly, sir, to speak with you.

FALSTAFF
Come, let me pour in some sack to the Thames water; for my belly's as cold as if I had swallowed snowballs for pills to cool the reins. Call her in.

BARDOLPH
Come in, woman.

[Enter MISTRESS QUICKLY.]

QUICKLY

By your leave. I cry you mercy. Give your worship good morrow.

FALSTAFF
Take away these chalices. Go, brew me a pottle of sack finely.

BARDOLPH
With eggs, sir?

FALSTAFF
Simple of itself; I'll no pullet-sperm in my brewage.

[Exit BARDOLPH.]

How now!

QUICKLY
Marry, sir, I come to your worship from Mistress Ford.

FALSTAFF
Mistress Ford! I have had ford enough; I was thrown into the ford; I have my belly full of ford.

QUICKLY
Alas the day! good heart, that was not her fault: she does so take on with her men; they mistook their erection.

FALSTAFF
So did I mine, to build upon a foolish woman's promise.

QUICKLY
Well, she laments, sir, for it, that it would yearn your heart to see it. Her husband goes this morning a-birding; she desires you once more to come to her between eight and nine; I must carry her word quickly. She'll make you amends, I warrant you.

FALSTAFF
Well, I will visit her. Tell her so; and bid her think what a man is; let her consider his frailty, and then judge of my merit.

QUICKLY
I will tell her.

FALSTAFF
Do so. Between nine and ten, sayest thou?

QUICKLY
Eight and nine, sir.

FALSTAFF
Well, be gone; I will not miss her.

QUICKLY
Peace be with you, sir.

[Exit MISTRESS QUICKLY.]

FALSTAFF
I marvel I hear not of Master Brook; he sent me word to stay within. I like his money well. O! here he comes.

[Enter FORD disguised.]

FORD
Bless you, sir!

FALSTAFF
Now, Master Brook, you come to know what hath passed between me and Ford's wife?

FORD
That, indeed, Sir John, is my business.

FALSTAFF
Master Brook, I will not lie to you: I was at her house the hour she appointed me.

FORD
And how sped you, sir?

FALSTAFF
Very ill-favouredly, Master Brook.

FORD
How so, sir? did she change her determination?

FALSTAFF
No. Master Brook; but the peaking cornuto her husband, Master Brook, dwelling in a continual 'larum of jealousy, comes me in the instant of our encounter, after we had embraced, kissed, protested, and, as it were, spoke the prologue of our comedy; and at his heels a rabble of his companions, thither provoked and instigated by his distemper, and, forsooth, to search his house for his wife's love.

FORD
What! while you were there?

FALSTAFF
While I was there.

FORD
And did he search for you, and could not find you?

FALSTAFF
You shall hear. As good luck would have it, comes in one Mistress Page;
gives intelligence of Ford's approach; and, in her invention and Ford's
wife's distraction, they conveyed me into a buck-basket.

FORD
A buck-basket!

FALSTAFF
By the Lord, a buck-basket! rammed me in with foul shirts and smocks,
socks, foul stockings, greasy napkins, that, Master Brook, there was the
rankest compound of villainous smell that ever offended nostril.

FORD
And how long lay you there?

FALSTAFF
Nay, you shall hear, Master Brook, what I have suffered to bring this
woman to evil for your good. Being thus crammed in the basket, a
couple of Ford's knaves, his hinds, were called forth by their mistress
to carry me in the name of foul clothes to Datchet-lane; they took me
on their shoulders; met the jealous knave their master in the door; who
asked them once or twice what they had in their basket. I quaked for
fear lest the lunatic knave would have searched it; but Fate, ordaining
he should be a cuckold, held his hand. Well, on went he for a search,
and away went I for foul clothes. But mark the sequel, Master Brook: I
suffered the pangs of three several deaths: first, an intolerable fright to be
detected with a jealous rotten bell-wether; next, to be compassed like a
good bilbo in the circumference of a peck, hilt to point, heel to head; and
then, to be stopped in, like a strong distillation, with stinking clothes that
fretted in their own grease: think of that; a man of my kidney, think of
that, that am as subject to heat as butter; a man of continual dissolution
and thaw: it was a miracle to 'scape suffocation. And in the height of this
bath, when I was more than half stewed in grease, like a Dutch dish, to
be thrown into the Thames, and cooled, glowing hot, in that surge, like a
horse-shoe; think of that, hissing hot, think of that, Master Brook!

FORD
In good sadness, sir, I am sorry that for my sake you have suffered all
this. My suit, then, is desperate; you'll undertake her no more.

FALSTAFF

Master Brook, I will be thrown into Etna, as I have been into Thames, ere I will leave her thus. Her husband is this morning gone a-birding; I have received from her another embassy of meeting; 'twixt eight and nine is the hour, Master Brook.

FORD

'Tis past eight already, sir.

FALSTAFF

Is it? I will then address me to my appointment. Come to me at your convenient leisure, and you shall know how I speed, and the conclusion shall be crowned with your enjoying her: adieu. You shall have her, Master Brook; Master Brook, you shall cuckold Ford.

[Exit FALSTAFF.]

FORD

Hum! ha! Is this a vision? Is this a dream? Do I sleep? Master Ford, awake; awake, Master Ford. There's a hole made in your best coat, Master Ford. This 'tis to be married; this 'tis to have linen and buck-baskets! Well, I will proclaim myself what I am; I will now take the lecher; he is at my house. He cannot scape me; 'tis impossible he should; he cannot creep into a half-penny purse, nor into a pepper box; but, lest the devil that guides him should aid him, I will search impossible places. Though what I am I cannot avoid, yet to be what I would not, shall not make me tame; if I have horns to make one mad, let the proverb go with me; I'll be horn-mad.

[Exit.]

ACT IV

SCENE I.

THE STREET

[Enter MISTRESS PAGE, MISTRESS QUICKLY, and WILLIAM.]

MRS. PAGE
Is he at Master Ford's already, think'st thou?

QUICKLY
Sure he is by this; or will be presently; but truly he is very courageous mad about his throwing into the water. Mistress Ford desires you to come suddenly.

MRS. PAGE
I'll be with her by and by; I'll but bring my young man here to school. Look where his master comes; 'tis a playing day, I see.

[Enter SIR HUGH EVANS.]

How now, Sir Hugh, no school to-day?

EVANS
No; Master Slender is let the boys leave to play.

QUICKLY
Blessing of his heart!

MRS. PAGE
Sir Hugh, my husband says my son profits nothing in the world at his book; I pray you ask him some questions in his accidence.

EVANS
Come hither, William; hold up your head; come.

MRS. PAGE
Come on, sirrah; hold up your head; answer your master; be not afraid.

EVANS
William, how many numbers is in nouns?

WILLIAM
Two.

QUICKLY
Truly, I thought there had been one number more, because they say
"Od's nouns."

EVANS
Peace your tattlings! What is "fair," William?

WILLIAM
Pulcher.

QUICKLY
Polecats! There are fairer things than polecats, sure.

EVANS
You are a very simplicity 'oman; I pray you, peace. What is "lapis," William?

WILLIAM
A stone.

EVANS
And what is "a stone," William?

WILLIAM
A pebble.

EVANS
No, it is "lapis"; I pray you remember in your prain.

WILLIAM
Lapis.

EVANS
That is a good William. What is he, William, that does lend articles?

WILLIAM
Articles are borrowed of the pronoun, and be thus declined: Singulariter,
nominativo; hic, haec, hoc.

EVANS
Nominativo, hig, hag, hog; pray you, mark: genitivo, hujus. Well, what is
your accusative case?

WILLIAM
Accusativo, hinc.

EVANS
I pray you, have your remembrance, child. Accusativo, hung, hang, hog.

QUICKLY
"Hang-hog" is Latin for bacon, I warrant you.

EVANS
Leave your prabbles, 'oman. What is the focative case, William?

WILLIAM
O vocativo, O.

EVANS
Remember, William: focative is caret.

QUICKLY
And that's a good root.

EVANS
'Oman, forbear.

MRS. PAGE
Peace.

EVANS
What is your genitive case plural, William?

WILLIAM
Genitive case?

EVANS
Ay.

WILLIAM
Genitive: horum, harum, horum.

QUICKLY
Vengeance of Jenny's case; fie on her! Never name her, child, if she be a whore.

EVANS
For shame, 'oman.

QUICKLY
You do ill to teach the child such words. He teaches him to hick and to hack, which they'll do fast enough of themselves; and to call "horum;" fie upon you!

EVANS
'Oman, art thou lunatics? Hast thou no understandings for thy cases, and the numbers of the genders? Thou art as foolish Christian creatures as I would desires.

MRS. PAGE
Prithee, hold thy peace.

EVANS
Show me now, William, some declensions of your pronouns.

WILLIAM
Forsooth, I have forgot.

EVANS
It is qui, quae, quod; if you forget your "quis", your "quaes", and your "quods", you must be preeches. Go your ways and play; go.

MRS. PAGE
He is a better scholar than I thought he was.

EVANS
He is a good sprag memory. Farewell, Mistress Page.

MRS. PAGE
Adieu, good Sir Hugh.

[Exit SIR HUGH.]

Get you home, boy. Come, we stay too long.

[Exeunt.]

SCENE II.

A ROOM IN FORD'S HOUSE

[Enter FALSTAFF and MISTRESS FORD.]

FALSTAFF
Mistress Ford, your sorrow hath eaten up my sufferance. I see you are obsequious in your love, and I profess requital to a hair's breadth; not only, Mistress Ford, in the simple office of love, but in all the accoutrement, complement, and ceremony of it. But are you sure of your husband now?

MRS. FORD
He's a-birding, sweet Sir John.

MRS. PAGE
[Within] What ho! gossip Ford, what ho!

MRS. FORD
Step into the chamber, Sir John.

[Exit FALSTAFF.]

[Enter MISTRESS PAGE.]

MRS. PAGE
How now, sweetheart! who's at home besides yourself?

MRS. FORD
Why, none but mine own people.

MRS. PAGE
Indeed!

MRS. FORD
No, certainly. —
[Aside to her] Speak louder.

MRS. PAGE
Truly, I am so glad you have nobody here.

MRS. FORD
Why?

MRS. PAGE
Why, woman, your husband is in his old lunes again. He so takes on
yonder with my husband; so rails against all married mankind; so curses
all Eve's daughters, of what complexion soever; and so buffets himself
on the forehead, crying "Peer out, peer out!" that any madness I ever yet
beheld seemed but tameness, civility, and patience, to this his distemper
he is in now. I am glad the fat knight is not here.

MRS. FORD
Why, does he talk of him?

MRS. PAGE
Of none but him; and swears he was carried out, the last time he
searched for him, in a basket; protests to my husband he is now here;
and hath drawn him and the rest of their company from their sport, to
make another experiment of his suspicion. But I am glad the knight is not
here; now he shall see his own foolery.

MRS. FORD
How near is he, Mistress Page?

MRS. PAGE
Hard by, at street end; he will be here anon.

MRS. FORD
I am undone! the knight is here.

MRS. PAGE
Why, then, you are utterly shamed, and he's but a dead man. What a
woman are you! Away with him, away with him! better shame than
murder.

MRS. FORD
Which way should he go? How should I bestow him? Shall I put him
into the basket again?

[Re-enter FALSTAFF.]

FALSTAFF
No, I'll come no more i' the basket. May I not go out ere he come?

MRS. PAGE
Alas! three of Master Ford's brothers watch the door with pistols, that

none shall issue out; otherwise you might slip away ere he came. But what make you here?

FALSTAFF
What shall I do? I'll creep up into the chimney.

MRS. FORD
There they always use to discharge their birding-pieces.

MRS. PAGE
Creep into the kiln-hole.

FALSTAFF
Where is it?

MRS. FORD
He will seek there, on my word. Neither press, coffer, chest, trunk, well, vault, but he hath an abstract for the remembrance of such places, and goes to them by his note: there is no hiding you in the house.

FALSTAFF
I'll go out then.

MRS. PAGE
If you go out in your own semblance, you die, Sir John. Unless you go out disguised, —

MRS. FORD
How might we disguise him?

MRS. PAGE
Alas the day! I know not! There is no woman's gown big enough for him; otherwise he might put on a hat, a muffler, and a kerchief, and so escape.

FALSTAFF
Good hearts, devise something: any extremity rather than a mischief.

MRS. FORD
My maid's aunt, the fat woman of Brainford, has a gown above.

MRS. PAGE
On my word, it will serve him; she's as big as he is; and there's her thrummed hat, and her muffler too. Run up, Sir John.

MRS. FORD
Go, go, sweet Sir John. Mistress Page and I will look some linen for your

head.

MRS. PAGE
Quick, quick! we'll come dress you straight; put on the gown the while.

[Exit FALSTAFF.]

MRS. FORD
I would my husband would meet him in this shape; he cannot abide the old woman of Brainford; he swears she's a witch, forbade her my house, and hath threatened to beat her.

MRS. PAGE
Heaven guide him to thy husband's cudgel; and the devil guide his cudgel afterwards!

MRS. FORD
But is my husband coming?

MRS. PAGE
Ay, in good sadness is he; and talks of the basket too, howsoever he hath had intelligence.

MRS. FORD
We'll try that; for I'll appoint my men to carry the basket again, to meet him at the door with it as they did last time.

MRS. PAGE
Nay, but he'll be here presently; let's go dress him like the witch of Brainford.

MRS. FORD
I'll first direct my men what they shall do with the basket. Go up; I'll bring linen for him straight.

[Exit MISTRESS FORD.]

MRS. PAGE
Hang him, dishonest varlet! we cannot misuse him enough.
We'll leave a proof, by that which we will do,
Wives may be merry and yet honest too.
We do not act that often jest and laugh;
'Tis old but true: "Still swine eats all the draff."

[Exit.]

[Re-enter MISTRESS FORD, with two SERVANTS.]

MRS. FORD
Go, sirs, take the basket again on your shoulders; your master is hard at

door; if he bid you set it down, obey him. Quickly, dispatch.

[Exit MISTRESS FORD.]

FIRST SERVANT
Come, come, take it up.

SECOND SERVANT
Pray heaven, it be not full of knight again.

FIRST SERVANT
I hope not; I had lief as bear so much lead.

[Enter FORD, PAGE, SHALLOW, CAIUS, and SIR HUGH EVANS.]

FORD
Ay, but if it prove true, Master Page, have you any way then to unfool
me again? Set down the basket, villain! Somebody call my wife. Youth in
a basket! O you panderly rascals! there's a knot, a ging, a pack, a conspir-
acy against me. Now shall the devil be shamed. What, wife, I say! Come,
come forth! behold what honest clothes you send forth to bleaching!

PAGE
Why, this passes, Master Ford! you are not to go loose any longer; you
must be pinioned.

EVANS
Why, this is lunatics! this is mad as a mad dog.

SHALLOW
Indeed, Master Ford, this is not well, indeed.

FORD
So say I too, sir. —

[Re-enter MISTRESS FORD.]

Come hither, Mistress Ford, the honest woman, the modest wife, the
virtuous creature, that hath the jealous fool to her husband! I suspect
without cause, Mistress, do I?

MRS. FORD
Heaven be my witness, you do, if you suspect me in any dishonesty.

FORD
Well said, brazen-face! hold it out. Come forth, sirrah. *[Pulling clothes out
of the basket]*

PAGE
This passes!

MRS. FORD
Are you not ashamed? Let the clothes alone.

FORD
I shall find you anon.

EVANS
'Tis unreasonable. Will you take up your wife's clothes? Come away.

FORD
Empty the basket, I say!

MRS. FORD
Why, man, why?

FORD
Master Page, as I am a man, there was one conveyed out of my house
yesterday in this basket: why may not he be there again? In my house I
am sure he is; my intelligence is true; my jealousy is reasonable. Pluck
me out all the linen.

MRS. FORD
If you find a man there, he shall die a flea's death.

PAGE
Here's no man.

SHALLOW
By my fidelity, this is not well, Master Ford; this wrongs you.

EVANS
Master Ford, you must pray, and not follow the imaginations of your
own heart; this is jealousies.

FORD
Well, he's not here I seek for.

PAGE
No, nor nowhere else but in your brain.

[Servants carry away the basket.]

FORD
Help to search my house this one time. If I find not what I seek, show no
colour for my extremity; let me for ever be your table-sport; let them say
of me "As jealous as Ford, that searched a hollow walnut for his wife's

leman." Satisfy me once more; once more search with me.

MRS. FORD
What, hoa, Mistress Page! Come you and the old woman down; my husband will come into the chamber.

FORD
Old woman? what old woman's that?

MRS. FORD
Why, it is my maid's aunt of Brainford.

FORD
A witch, a quean, an old cozening quean! Have I not forbid her my house? She comes of errands, does she? We are simple men; we do not know what's brought to pass under the profession of fortune-telling. She works by charms, by spells, by the figure, and such daubery as this is, beyond our element. We know nothing. Come down, you witch, you hag you; come down, I say!

MRS. FORD
Nay, good sweet husband! Good gentlemen, let him not strike the old woman.

[Re-enter FALSTAFF in woman's clothes, led by MISTRESS PAGE.]

MRS. PAGE
Come, Mother Prat; come, give me your hand.

FORD
I'll prat her. — *[Beats him.]* Out of my door, you witch, you rag, you baggage, you polecat, you ronyon! Out, out! I'll conjure you, I'll fortune-tell you.

[Exit FALSTAFF.]

MRS. PAGE
Are you not ashamed? I think you have killed the poor woman.

MRS. FORD
Nay, he will do it. 'Tis a goodly credit for you.

FORD
Hang her, witch!

EVANS. By yea and no, I think the 'oman is a witch indeed; I like not when a 'oman has a great peard; I spy a great peard under her muffler.

FORD

Will you follow, gentlemen? I beseech you follow; see but the issue of my jealousy; if I cry out thus upon no trail, never trust me when I open again.

PAGE
Let's obey his humour a little further. Come, gentlemen.

[Exeunt FORD, PAGE, SHALLOW, CAIUS, and EVANS.]

MRS. PAGE
Trust me, he beat him most pitifully.

MRS. FORD
Nay, by the mass, that he did not; he beat him most unpitifully methought.

MRS. PAGE
I'll have the cudgel hallowed and hung o'er the altar; it hath done meritorious service.

MRS. FORD
What think you? May we, with the warrant of womanhood and the witness of a good conscience, pursue him with any further revenge?

MRS. PAGE. The spirit of wantonness is sure scared out of him; if the devil have him not in fee-simple, with fine and recovery, he will never, I think, in the way of waste, attempt us again.

MRS. FORD
Shall we tell our husbands how we have served him?

MRS. PAGE
Yes, by all means; if it be but to scrape the figures out of your husband's brains. If they can find in their hearts the poor unvirtuous fat knight shall be any further afflicted, we two will still be the ministers.

MRS. FORD
I'll warrant they'll have him publicly shamed; and methinks there would be no period to the jest, should he not be publicly shamed.

MRS. PAGE
Come, to the forge with it then; shape it. I would not have things cool.

[Exeunt.]

SCENE III.

A ROOM IN THE GARTER INN

[Enter HOST and BARDOLPH.]

BARDOLPH
Sir, the Germans desire to have three of your horses; the Duke himself
will be to-morrow at court, and they are going to meet him.

HOST
What duke should that be comes so secretly? I hear not of him in the
court. Let me speak with the gentlemen; they speak English?

BARDOLPH
Ay, sir; I'll call them to you.

HOST
They shall have my horses, but I'll make them pay; I'll sauce them; they
have had my house a week at command; I have turned away my other
guests. They must come off; I'll sauce them. Come.

[Exeunt.]

SCENE IV.

A ROOM IN FORD'S HOUSE

[Enter PAGE, FORD, MISTRESS PAGE, MISTRESS FORD, and SIR HUGH EVANS.]

EVANS
'Tis one of the best discretions of a 'oman as ever I did look upon.

PAGE
And did he send you both these letters at an instant?

MRS. PAGE
Within a quarter of an hour.

FORD
Pardon me, wife. Henceforth, do what thou wilt;
I rather will suspect the sun with cold
Than thee with wantonness: now doth thy honour stand,
In him that was of late an heretic,
As firm as faith.

PAGE
'Tis well, 'tis well; no more.
Be not as extreme in submission
As in offence;
But let our plot go forward: let our wives
Yet once again, to make us public sport,
Appoint a meeting with this old fat fellow,
Where we may take him and disgrace him for it.

FORD
There is no better way than that they spoke of.

PAGE
How? To send him word they'll meet him in the park at midnight? Fie, fie! he'll never come!

EVANS

You say he has been thrown in the rivers; and has been grievously peaten as an old 'oman; methinks there should be terrors in him, that he should not come; methinks his flesh is punished; he shall have no desires.

PAGE
So think I too.

MRS. FORD
Devise but how you'll use him when he comes,
And let us two devise to bring him thither.

MRS. PAGE
There is an old tale goes that Herne the hunter,
Sometime a keeper here in Windsor Forest,
Doth all the winter-time, at still midnight,
Walk round about an oak, with great ragg'd horns;
And there he blasts the tree, and takes the cattle,
And makes milch-kine yield blood, and shakes a chain
In a most hideous and dreadful manner:
You have heard of such a spirit, and well you know
The superstitious idle-headed eld
Received, and did deliver to our age,
This tale of Herne the hunter for a truth.

PAGE
Why, yet there want not many that do fear
In deep of night to walk by this Herne's oak.
But what of this?

MRS. FORD
Marry, this is our device;
That Falstaff at that oak shall meet with us,
Disguis'd, like Herne, with huge horns on his head.

PAGE
Well, let it not be doubted but he'll come,
And in this shape. When you have brought him thither,
What shall be done with him? What is your plot?

MRS. PAGE
That likewise have we thought upon, and thus:
Nan Page my daughter, and my little son,
And three or four more of their growth, we'll dress
Like urchins, ouphs, and fairies, green and white,
With rounds of waxen tapers on their heads,
And rattles in their hands. Upon a sudden,

As Falstaff, she, and I, are newly met,
Let them from forth a sawpit rush at once
With some diffusèd song; upon their sight
We two in great amazèdness will fly:
Then let them all encircle him about,
And fairy-like, to pinch the unclean knight;
And ask him why, that hour of fairy revel,
In their so sacred paths he dares to tread
In shape profane.

MRS. FORD
And till he tell the truth,
Let the supposèd fairies pinch him sound,
And burn him with their tapers.

MRS. PAGE
The truth being known,
We'll all present ourselves; dis-horn the spirit,
And mock him home to Windsor.

FORD
The children must
Be practis'd well to this or they'll ne'er do 't.

EVANS
I will teach the children their behaviours; and I will be like a jack-an-apes
also, to burn the knight with my taber.

FORD
That will be excellent. I'll go buy them vizards.

MRS. PAGE
My Nan shall be the Queen of all the Fairies,
Finely attired in a robe of white.

PAGE
That silk will I go buy.
[Aside] And in that time
Shall Master Slender steal my Nan away,
And marry her at Eton. Go, send to Falstaff straight.

FORD
Nay, I'll to him again, in name of Brook;
He'll tell me all his purpose. Sure, he'll come.

MRS. PAGE

Fear not you that. Go, get us properties
And tricking for our fairies.

EVANS
Let us about it. It is admirable pleasures, and fery honest knaveries.

[Exeunt PAGE, FORD, and EVANS.]

MRS. PAGE
Go, Mistress Ford.
Send Quickly to Sir John to know his mind.

[Exit MRS. FORD.]

I'll to the Doctor; he hath my good will,
And none but he, to marry with Nan Page.
That Slender, though well landed, is an idiot;
And he my husband best of all affects:
The Doctor is well money'd, and his friends
Potent at court: he, none but he, shall have her,
Though twenty thousand worthier come to crave her.

[Exit.]

SCENE V.

A ROOM IN THE GARTER INN

[Enter HOST and SIMPLE.]

HOST
What wouldst thou have, boor? What, thick-skin? Speak, breathe, discuss; brief, short, quick, snap.

SIMPLE
Marry, sir, I come to speak with Sir John Falstaff from Master Slender.

HOST
There's his chamber, his house, his castle, his standing-bed and truckle-bed; 'tis painted about with the story of the Prodigal, fresh and new. Go knock and call; he'll speak like an Anthropophaginian unto thee; knock, I say.

SIMPLE
There's an old woman, a fat woman, gone up into his chamber; I'll be so bold as stay, sir, till she come down; I come to speak with her, indeed.

HOST
Ha! a fat woman? The knight may be robbed. I'll call. Bully knight! Bully Sir John! Speak from thy lungs military. Art thou there? It is thine host, thine Ephesian, calls.

FALSTAFF
[Above] How now, mine host?

HOST
Here's a Bohemian-Tartar tarries the coming down of thy fat woman. Let her descend, bully, let her descend; my chambers are honourible. Fie! privacy? fie!

[Enter FALSTAFF.]

FALSTAFF
There was, mine host, an old fat woman even now with, me; but she's gone.

SIMPLE
Pray you, sir, was't not the wise woman of Brainford?

FALSTAFF
Ay, marry was it, mussel-shell: what would you with her?

SIMPLE
My master, sir, my Master Slender, sent to her, seeing her go thorough the streets, to know, sir, whether one Nym, sir, that beguiled him of a chain, had the chain or no.

FALSTAFF
I spake with the old woman about it.

SIMPLE
And what says she, I pray, sir?

FALSTAFF
Marry, she says that the very same man that beguiled Master Slender of his chain cozened him of it.

SIMPLE
I would I could have spoken with the woman herself; I had other things to have spoken with her too, from him.

FALSTAFF
What are they? Let us know.

HOST
Ay, come; quick.

SIMPLE
I may not conceal them, sir.

FALSTAFF
Conceal them, or thou diest.

SIMPLE
Why, sir, they were nothing but about Mistress Anne Page: to know if it were my master's fortune to have her or no.

FALSTAFF
'Tis, 'tis his fortune.

SIMPLE

What sir?

FALSTAFF
To have her, or no. Go; say the woman told me so.

SIMPLE
May I be bold to say so, sir?

FALSTAFF
Ay, Sir Tike; like who more bold?

SIMPLE
I thank your worship; I shall make my master glad with these tidings.

[Exit SIMPLE.]

HOST
Thou art clerkly, thou art clerkly, Sir John. Was there a wise woman with
thee?

FALSTAFF
Ay, that there was, mine host; one that hath taught me more wit than
ever I learned before in my life; and I paid nothing for it neither, but was
paid for my learning.

[Enter BARDOLPH.]

BARDOLPH
Out, alas, sir! cozenage, mere cozenage!

HOST
Where be my horses? Speak well of them, varletto.

BARDOLPH
Run away, with the cozeners; for so soon as I came beyond Eton, they
threw me off, from behind one of them, in a slough of mire; and set spurs
and away, like three German devils, three Doctor Faustuses.

HOST
They are gone but to meet the Duke, villain; do not say they be fled; Germans are honest men.

[Enter SIR HUGH EVANS.]

EVANS
Where is mine host?

HOST
What is the matter, sir?

EVANS
Have a care of your entertainments: there is a friend of mine come to
town tells me there is three cozen-germans that has cozened all the hosts
of Readins, of Maidenhead, of Colebrook, of horses and money. I tell
you for good will, look you; you are wise, and full of gibes and vlout-
ing-stogs, and 'tis not convenient you should be cozened. Fare you well.

[Exit EVANS.]

[Enter DOCTOR CAIUS.]

CAIUS
Vere is mine host de Jarteer?

HOST
Here, Master Doctor, in perplexity and doubtful dilemma.

CAIUS
I cannot tell vat is dat; but it is tell-a me dat you make grand preparation
for a Duke de Jamany. By my trot, dere is no duke that the court is know
to come; I tell you for good will: Adieu.

[Exit DOCTOR CAIUS.]

HOST
Hue and cry, villain, go! Assist me, knight; I am undone. Fly, run, hue
and cry, villain; I am undone!

[Exeunt HOST and BARDOLPH.]

FALSTAFF
I would all the world might be cozened, for I have been cozened and
beaten too. If it should come to the ear of the court how I have been
transformed, and how my transformation hath been washed and cud-
gelled, they would melt me out of my fat, drop by drop, and liquor
fishermen's boots with me; I warrant they would whip me with their fine
wits till I were as crest-fallen as a dried pear. I never prospered since I
forswore myself at primero. Well, if my wind were but long enough to
say my prayers, I would repent.

[Enter MISTRESS QUICKLY.]

Now! whence come you?

QUICKLY
From the two parties, forsooth.

FALSTAFF
The devil take one party and his dam the other! And so they shall be
both bestowed. I have suffered more for their sakes, more than the villainous inconstancy of man's disposition is able to bear.

QUICKLY
And have not they suffered? Yes, I warrant; speciously one of them;
Mistress Ford, good heart, is beaten black and blue, that you cannot see a
white spot about her.

FALSTAFF
What tellest thou me of black and blue? I was beaten myself into all the
colours of the rainbow; and was like to be apprehended for the witch of
Brainford. But that my admirable dexterity of wit, my counterfeiting the
action of an old woman, delivered me, the knave constable had set me i'
the stocks, i' the common stocks, for a witch.

QUICKLY
Sir, let me speak with you in your chamber; you shall hear how things
go, and, I warrant, to your content. Here is a letter will say somewhat.
Good hearts, what ado here is to bring you together! Sure, one of you
does not serve heaven well, that you are so crossed.

FALSTAFF
Come up into my chamber.

[Exeunt.]

SCENE VI.

ANOTHER ROOM IN THE GARTER INN

[Enter FENTON and HOST.]

HOST
Master Fenton, talk not to me; my mind is heavy; I will give over all.

FENTON
Yet hear me speak. Assist me in my purpose,
And, as I am a gentleman, I'll give thee
A hundred pound in gold more than your loss.

HOST
I will hear you, Master Fenton; and I will, at the least, keep your counsel.

FENTON
From time to time I have acquainted you
With the dear love I bear to fair Anne Page,
Who, mutually, hath answered my affection,
So far forth as herself might be her chooser,
Even to my wish. I have a letter from her
Of such contents as you will wonder at;
The mirth whereof so larded with my matter
That neither, singly, can be manifested
Without the show of both; wherein fat Falstaff
Hath a great scare: the image of the jest
I'll show you here at large. Hark, good mine host:
To-night at Herne's oak, just 'twixt twelve and one,
Must my sweet Nan present the Fairy Queen;
The purpose why is here: in which disguise,
While other jests are something rank on foot,
Her father hath commanded her to slip
Away with Slender, and with him at Eton
Immediately to marry; she hath consented:
Now, sir,
Her mother, even strong against that match
And firm for Doctor Caius, hath appointed
That he shall likewise shuffle her away,

While other sports are tasking of their minds;
And at the deanery, where a priest attends,
Straight marry her: to this her mother's plot
She seemingly obedient likewise hath
Made promise to the doctor. Now thus it rests:
Her father means she shall be all in white;
And in that habit, when Slender sees his time
To take her by the hand and bid her go,
She shall go with him: her mother hath intended
The better to denote her to the doctor, —
For they must all be mask'd and vizarded —
That quaint in green she shall be loose enrob'd,
With ribands pendent, flaring 'bout her head;
And when the doctor spies his vantage ripe,
To pinch her by the hand: and, on that token,
The maid hath given consent to go with him.

HOST
Which means she to deceive, father or mother?

FENTON
Both, my good host, to go along with me:
And here it rests, that you'll procure the vicar
To stay for me at church, 'twixt twelve and one,
And in the lawful name of marrying,
To give our hearts united ceremony.

HOST
Well, husband your device; I'll to the vicar.
Bring you the maid, you shall not lack a priest.

FENTON
So shall I evermore be bound to thee;
Besides, I'll make a present recompense.

[Exeunt.]

ACT V

SCENE I.

A ROOM IN THE GARTER INN

[Enter FALSTAFF and MISTRESS QUICKLY.]

FALSTAFF
Prithee, no more prattling; go: I'll hold. This is the third time; I hope
good luck lies in odd numbers. Away! go. They say there is divinity in
odd numbers, either in nativity, chance, or death. Away!

QUICKLY
I'll provide you a chain, and I'll do what I can to get you a pair of horns.

FALSTAFF
Away, I say; time wears; hold up your head, and mince.

[Exit MRS. QUICKLY.]

[Enter FORD.]

How now, Master Brook! Master Brook, the matter will be known to-
night, or never. Be you in the Park about midnight, at Herne's oak, and
you shall see wonders.

FORD
Went you not to her yesterday, sir, as you told me you had appointed?

FALSTAFF
I went to her, Master Brook, as you see, like a poor old man; but I came
from her, Master Brook, like a poor old woman. That same knave Ford,
her husband, hath the finest mad devil of jealousy in him, Master Brook,
that ever governed frenzy. I will tell you: he beat me grievously in the
shape of a woman; for in the shape of man, Master Brook, I fear not
Goliath with a weaver's beam, because I know also life is a shuttle. I am
in haste; go along with me; I'll tell you all, Master Brook. Since I plucked
geese, played truant, and whipped top, I knew not what 'twas to be beat-
en till lately. Follow me: I'll tell you strange things of this knave Ford, on
whom to-night I will be revenged, and I will deliver his wife into your
hand. Follow. Strange things in hand, Master Brook! Follow.

[Exeunt.]

SCENE II.

WINDSOR PARK

[*Enter PAGE, SHALLOW, and SLENDER.*]

PAGE
Come, come; we'll couch i' the castle-ditch till we see the light of our fairies. Remember, son Slender, my daughter.

SLENDER
Ay, forsooth; I have spoke with her, and we have a nay-word how to know one another. I come to her in white and cry "mum"; she cries "budget," and by that we know one another.

SHALLOW
That's good too; but what needs either your "mum" or her "budget"? The white will decipher her well enough. It hath struck ten o'clock.

PAGE
The night is dark; light and spirits will become it well. Heaven prosper our sport! No man means evil but the devil, and we shall know him by his horns. Let's away; follow me.

[*Exeunt.*]

SCENE III.

THE STREET IN WINDSOR

[Enter MISTRESS PAGE, MISTRESS FORD, and DOCTOR CAIUS.]

MRS. PAGE
Master Doctor, my daughter is in green; when you see your time, take her by the hand, away with her to the deanery, and dispatch it quickly. Go before into the Park; we two must go together.

CAIUS
I know vat I have to do; adieu.

MRS. PAGE
Fare you well, sir.

[Exit CAIUS.]

My husband will not rejoice so much at the abuse of Falstaff as he will chafe at the doctor's marrying my daughter; but 'tis no matter; better a little chiding than a great deal of heart break.

MRS. FORD
Where is Nan now, and her troop of fairies, and the Welsh devil, Hugh?

MRS. PAGE
They are all couched in a pit hard by Herne's oak, with obscured lights; which, at the very instant of Falstaff's and our meeting, they will at once display to the night.

MRS. FORD
That cannot choose but amaze him.

MRS. PAGE
If he be not amazed, he will be mocked; if he be amazed, he will every way be mocked.

MRS. FORD
We'll betray him finely.

MRS. PAGE
Against such lewdsters and their lechery,
Those that betray them do no treachery.

MRS. FORD
The hour draws on: to the oak, to the oak!

[Exeunt.]

SCENE IV.

WINDSOR PARK

[Enter SIR HUGH EVANS, disguised, with others as Fairies.]

EVANS
Trib, trib, fairies; come; and remember your parts. Be pold, I pray you; follow me into the pit; and when I give the watch-ords, do as I pid you. Come, come; trib, trib.

[Exeunt.]

SCENE V.

ANOTHER PART OF THE PARK

[Enter FALSTAFF disguised as HERNE with a buck's head on.]

FALSTAFF
The Windsor bell hath struck twelve; the minute draws on. Now the hot-blooded gods assist me! Remember, Jove, thou wast a bull for thy Europa; love set on thy horns. O powerful love! that in some respects, makes a beast a man; in some other a man a beast. You were also, Jupiter, a swan, for the love of Leda. O omnipotent love! how near the god drew to the complexion of a goose! A fault done first in the form of a beast; O Jove, a beastly fault! and then another fault in the semblance of a fowl: think on't, Jove, a foul fault! When gods have hot backs what shall poor men do? For me, I am here a Windsor stag; and the fattest, I think, i' the forest. Send me a cool rut-time, Jove, or who can blame me to piss my tallow? Who comes here? my doe?

[Enter MISTRESS FORD and MISTRESS PAGE.]

MRS. FORD
Sir John! Art thou there, my deer? my male deer?

FALSTAFF
My doe with the black scut! Let the sky rain potatoes; let it thunder to the tune of "Greensleeves"; hail kissing-comfits and snow eringoes; let there come a tempest of provocation, I will shelter me here.

[Embracing her]

MRS. FORD
Mistress Page is come with me, sweetheart.

FALSTAFF
Divide me like a brib'd buck, each a haunch; I will keep my sides to myself, my shoulders for the fellow of this walk, and my horns I bequeath your husbands. Am I a woodman, ha? Speak I like Herne the hunter? Why, now is Cupid a child of conscience; he makes restitution. As I am a true spirit, welcome!

[Noise within]

MRS. PAGE

Alas! what noise?

MRS. FORD
Heaven forgive our sins!

FALSTAFF
What should this be?

MRS. FORD
Away, away!

MRS. PAGE
Away, away!

[They run off.]

FALSTAFF
I think the devil will not have me damned, lest the oil that's in me should set hell on fire; he would never else cross me thus.

[Enter SIR HUGH EVANS like a Satyr, PISTOL as a Hobgoblin, ANNE PAGE as the the Fairy Queen, attended by her Brothers and Others, as fairies, with waxen tapers on their heads.]

ANNE
Fairies, black, grey, green, and white,
You moonshine revellers, and shades of night,
You orphan heirs of fixèd destiny,
Attend your office and your quality.
Crier Hobgoblin, make the fairy oyes.

PISTOL
Elves, list your names: silence, you airy toys!
Cricket, to Windsor chimneys shalt thou leap:
Where fires thou find'st unrak'd, and hearths unswept,
There pinch the maids as blue as bilberry:
Our radiant Queen hates sluts and sluttery.

FALSTAFF
They are fairies; he that speaks to them shall die:
I'll wink and couch: no man their works must eye.

[Lies down upon his face.]

EVANS
Where's Bede? Go you, and where you find a maid
That, ere she sleep, has thrice her prayers said,
Rein up the organs of her fantasy,
Sleep she as sound as careless infancy;
But those as sleep and think not on their sins,

Pinch them, arms, legs, backs, shoulders, sides, and shins.

ANNE
About, about!
Search Windsor castle, elves, within and out:
Strew good luck, ouphes, on every sacred room,
That it may stand till the perpetual doom,
In state as wholesome as in state 'tis fit,
Worthy the owner and the owner it.
The several chairs of order look you scour
With juice of balm and every precious flower:
Each fair instalment, coat, and several crest,
With loyal blazon, evermore be blest!
And nightly, meadow-fairies, look you sing,
Like to the Garter's compass, in a ring:
The expressure that it bears, green let it be,
More fertile-fresh than all the field to see;
And "Honi soit qui mal y pense" write
In emerald tufts, flowers purple, blue and white;
Like sapphire, pearl, and rich embroidery,
Buckled below fair knighthood's bending knee.
Fairies use flowers for their charactery.
Away! disperse! But, till 'tis one o'clock,
Our dance of custom round about the oak
Of Herne the hunter let us not forget.

EVANS
Pray you, lock hand in hand; yourselves in order set;
And twenty glow-worms shall our lanterns be,
To guide our measure round about the tree.
But, stay; I smell a man of middle-earth.

FALSTAFF
Heavens defend me from that Welsh fairy, lest he transform me to a
piece of cheese!

PISTOL
Vile worm, thou wast o'erlook'd even in thy birth.

ANNE
With trial-fire touch me his finger-end:
If he be chaste, the flame will back descend
And turn him to no pain; but if he start,
It is the flesh of a corrupted heart.

PISTOL

A trial! come.

EVANS
Come, will this wood take fire?

[They burn him with their tapers.]

FALSTAFF
Oh, oh, oh!

ANNE
Corrupt, corrupt, and tainted in desire!
About him, fairies; sing a scornful rhyme;
And, as you trip, still pinch him to your time.

SONG.

Fie on sinful fantasy!
Fie on lust and luxury!
Lust is but a bloody fire,
Kindled with unchaste desire,
Fed in heart, whose flames aspire,
As thoughts do blow them, higher and higher.
Pinch him, fairies, mutually;
Pinch him for his villany;
Pinch him and burn him and turn him about,
Till candles and star-light and moonshine be out.

*[During this song the Fairies pinch FALSTAFF. DOCTOR CAIUS comes one
way, and steals away a fairy in green; SLENDER another way, and takes off a
fairy in white; and FENTON comes, and steals away ANNE PAGE. A noise
of hunting is heard within. All the fairies run away. FALSTAFF pulls off his
buck's head, and rises.]*

*[Enter PAGE, FORD, MISTRESS PAGE, MISTRESS FORD. They lay hold
on FALSTAFF.]*

PAGE
Nay, do not fly; I think we have watch'd you now:
Will none but Herne the hunter serve your turn?

MRS. PAGE
I pray you, come, hold up the jest no higher.
Now, good Sir John, how like you Windsor wives?
See you these, husband? do not these fair yokes
Become the forest better than the town?

FORD
Now, sir, who's a cuckold now? Master Brook, Falstaff's a knave, a

cuckoldly knave; here are his horns, Master Brook; and, Master Brook, he hath enjoyed nothing of Ford's but his buck-basket, his cudgel, and twenty pounds of money, which must be paid to Master Brook; his horses are arrested for it, Master Brook.

MRS. FORD
Sir John, we have had ill luck; we could never meet. I will never take you for my love again; but I will always count you my deer.

FALSTAFF
I do begin to perceive that I am made an ass.

FORD
Ay, and an ox too; both the proofs are extant.

FALSTAFF
And these are not fairies? I was three or four times in the thought they were not fairies; and yet the guiltiness of my mind, the sudden surprise of my powers, drove the grossness of the foppery into a received belief, in despite of the teeth of all rhyme and reason, that they were fairies. See now how wit may be made a Jack-a-Lent when 'tis upon ill employment!

EVANS
Sir John Falstaff, serve Got, and leave your desires, and fairies will not pinse you.

FORD
Well said, fairy Hugh.

EVANS
And leave you your jealousies too, I pray you.

FORD
I will never mistrust my wife again, till thou art able to woo her in good English.

FALSTAFF
Have I laid my brain in the sun, and dried it, that it wants matter to prevent so gross o'er-reaching as this? Am I ridden with a Welsh goat too? Shall I have a cox-comb of frieze? 'Tis time I were choked with a piece of toasted cheese.

EVANS
Seese is not good to give putter: your belly is all putter.

FALSTAFF

"Seese" and "putter"! Have I lived to stand at the taunt of one that makes fritters of English? This is enough to be the decay of lust and late-walking through the realm.

MRS. PAGE
Why, Sir John, do you think, though we would have thrust virtue out of our hearts by the head and shoulders, and have given ourselves without scruple to hell, that ever the devil could have made you our delight?

FORD
What, a hodge-pudding? a bag of flax?

MRS. PAGE
A puffed man?

PAGE
Old, cold, withered, and of intolerable entrails?

FORD
And one that is as slanderous as Satan?

PAGE
And as poor as Job?

FORD
And as wicked as his wife?

EVANS
And given to fornications, and to taverns, and sack and wine, and metheglins, and to drinkings and swearings and starings, pribbles and prabbles?

FALSTAFF
Well, I am your theme; you have the start of me; I am dejected; I am not able to answer the Welsh flannel. Ignorance itself is a plummet o'er me; use me as you will.

FORD
Marry, sir, we'll bring you to Windsor, to one Master Brook, that you have cozened of money, to whom you should have been a pander: over and above that you have suffered, I think to repay that money will be a biting affliction.

MRS. FORD
Nay, husband, let that go to make amends;
Forget that sum, so we'll all be friends.

FORD
Well, here's my hand: all is forgiven at last.

PAGE
Yet be cheerful, knight; thou shalt eat a posset tonight at my house;
where I will desire thee to laugh at my wife, that now laughs at thee. Tell
her, Master Slender hath married her daughter.

MRS. PAGE
[Aside] Doctors doubt that; if Anne Page be my daughter, she is, by this,
Doctor Caius' wife.

[Enter SLENDER.]

SLENDER
Whoa, ho! ho! father Page!

PAGE
Son, how now! how now, son! have you dispatched?

SLENDER
Dispatched! I'll make the best in Gloucestershire know on't; would I
were hanged, la, else!

PAGE
Of what, son?

SLENDER
I came yonder at Eton to marry Mistress Anne Page, and she's a great
lubberly boy: if it had not been i' the church, I would have swinged him,
or he should have swinged me. If I did not think it had been Anne Page,
would I might never stir! and 'tis a postmaster's boy.

PAGE
Upon my life, then, you took the wrong.

SLENDER
What need you tell me that? I think so, when I took a boy for a girl. If I
had been married to him, for all he was in woman's apparel, I would not
have had him.

PAGE
Why, this is your own folly. Did not I tell you how you should know my
daughter by her garments?

SLENDER

I went to her in white and cried "mum" and she cried "budget" as Anne
and I had appointed; and yet it was not Anne, but a postmaster's boy.

EVANS
Jeshu! Master Slender, cannot you see put marry poys?

PAGE
O I am vexed at heart: what shall I do?

MRS. PAGE
Good George, be not angry: I knew of your purpose; turned my daughter
into green; and, indeed, she is now with the doctor at the deanery, and
there married.

[Enter DOCTOR CAIUS.]

CAIUS
Vere is Mistress Page? By gar, I am cozened; I ha' married un garçon, a
boy; un paysan, by gar, a boy; it is not Anne Page; by gar, I am cozened.

MRS. PAGE
Why, did you take her in green?

CAIUS
Ay, by gar, and 'tis a boy: by gar, I'll raise all Windsor.

[Exit DOCTOR CAIUS.]

FORD
This is strange. Who hath got the right Anne?

PAGE
My heart misgives me; here comes Master Fenton.

[Enter FENTON and ANNE PAGE.]

How now, Master Fenton!

ANNE
Pardon, good father! good my mother, pardon!

PAGE
Now, Mistress, how chance you went not with Master Slender?

MRS. PAGE
Why went you not with Master Doctor, maid?

FENTON
You do amaze her: hear the truth of it.
You would have married her most shamefully,

Where there was no proportion held in love.
The truth is, she and I, long since contracted,
Are now so sure that nothing can dissolve us.
The offence is holy that she hath committed,
And this deceit loses the name of craft,
Of disobedience, or unduteous title,
Since therein she doth evitate and shun
A thousand irreligious cursèd hours,
Which forcèd marriage would have brought upon her.

FORD
Stand not amaz'd: here is no remedy:
In love, the heavens themselves do guide the state:
Money buys lands, and wives are sold by fate.

FALSTAFF
I am glad, though you have ta'en a special stand to strike at me, that your
arrow hath glanced.

PAGE
Well, what remedy? — Fenton, heaven give thee joy!
What cannot be eschew'd must be embrac'd.

FALSTAFF
When night-dogs run, all sorts of deer are chas'd.

MRS. PAGE
Well, I will muse no further. Master Fenton,
Heaven give you many, many merry days!
Good husband, let us every one go home,
And laugh this sport o'er by a country fire;
Sir John and all.

FORD
Let it be so. Sir John,
To Master Brook you yet shall hold your word;
For he, to-night, shall lie with Mistress Ford.

[Exeunt.]

Lector House believes that a society develops through a two-fold approach of continuous learning and adaptation, which is derived from the study of classic literary works spread across the historic timeline of literature records. Therefore, we aim at reviving, repairing and redeveloping all those inaccessible or damaged but historically as well as culturally important literature across subjects so that the future generations may have an opportunity to study and learn from past works to embark upon a journey of creating a better future.

This book is a result of an effort made by Lector House towards making a contribution to the preservation and repair of original ancient works which might hold historical significance to the approach of continuous learning across subjects.

HAPPY READING & LEARNING!

LECTOR HOUSE LLP
E-MAIL: lectorpublishing@gmail.com

9 789353 443009

CPSIA information can be obtained
at www.ICGtesting.com
Printed in the USA
BVHW031939040819
555064BV00003B/924/P